SQL

Easy SQL Programming & Database Management For Beginners

Your Step-By-Step Guide To Learning The SQL Database.

Felix Alvaro

Acknowledgments

Firstly, I want to thank God for giving me the knowledge and inspiration to put this informative book together. I also want to thank my parents, my brothers and my partner Silvia for their support.

Table of Contents

Acknowledgments 2

Table of Contents 3

Introduction 5

Chapter One: SQL Overview 7

Chapter Two: The Database Essentials 12

Chapter Three: The SQL Structure 21

Chapter Four: Data Types 44

Chapter Five: Data Definition Language Statements 55

Chapter Six: Data Manipulation Language Statements 67

Chapter Seven: Data Query Language Statements 102

Chapter Eight: Transactional Control Commands 118

Chapter Nine: Database Views 138

Chapter Ten: Enhancing Database Designs 153

Chapter Eleven: Database Advance Topics 170

Chapter Twelve: Exercises 178

Exercise Answers 182

Final Words 187

© Copyright 2017 by D.A.Alvaro - All rights reserved.

This document is geared towards providing exact and reliable information in regard to the topic and issue covered.

It is not legal to reproduce, duplicate, or transmit any part of this document in either electronic means or in printed format. Recording of this publication is strictly prohibited.

Introduction

Hi there! Thank you so much for downloading this eBook on SQL Programming and Database Management for Beginners. I assure you that you have made a wise decision in investing in your skills as a database professional. This eBook will teach you vital information on the fundamentals of database programming and management using one of the powerful software tools – the SQL language. I am Felix, who also started as a simple analyst and I am now progressing into becoming a database scientist.

Through the guidance of this eBook, you will have a better understanding of the countless opportunities that this SQL language can bring you. I will be presenting you step-by-step instructions in learning the essential skills of this reliable database software.

At first, I did not realize how important it is for one to comprehend SQL, since there are other program applications you can use, such as Microsoft Excel, to process and present information. When I started researching the value of SQL, I told myself that if I continue embarking on this field then I will not just be presenting information but analyzing data as well. After downloading and installing the software, I have found out that it is not that challenging to study SQL programming after all!

Taking that first step to understanding the basic database concepts will lead you to expanding your knowledge and becoming one of the most sought-after IT professionals.

The current trend in information technology is to be more digital, which entails manipulating databases. This is where SQL comes into place – a software language that is powerful, yet simple, flexible, portable and, most of all, integrated into numerous database applications.

Deciding to become a database professional will definitely promise you a secured job with a potential high remuneration. On the average, a simple database analyst in the United States earns an annual salary of around $92,000 USD.

To start your journey in this field of database programming and management, let this eBook serve as your initial guide in educating yourself with the basics of SQL.

I will provide you an overview of how the language started, the various features of the software and its environment, the different commands and functions, the available error-handling tools, some advanced topics and much more! My ultimate aim is for you to appreciate the potentials of SQL and grasp the programming concepts in a cool way.

What are you waiting for?

Let us get started!

Chapter One: SQL Overview

In this chapter, you will learn a brief background on how and why SQL came into existence. Gaining knowledge on the history of this computer language will help you understand its importance to most IT professionals who focus on the field of data manipulation. You will also have an idea on how to maximize the potentials of SQL in the ever-changing world of Information Technology.

The current trend in most businesses today is to invest in technology that will gather data in the most efficient and effective way. However, gathering information is only the start of the extensive process of data manipulation. Companies, especially multi-national ones, require experts who possess the skills of analyzing, presenting, managing and storing data. In other words, they need to use computer programs that will transform raw company data to useful information. Now, thanks to *Structured Query Language*, or simply *SQL*, data scientists brought about such transformation in accessing and manipulating data in a very meaningful way.

History of SQL

Pronounced as *ees-que-ell* or *see'qwl*, SQL is a computer language initially invented by an American multinational technology and consulting company known as IBM (International Business Machines Corporation) way back in the 1970s using Dr. E. F. Codd's paper on "A Relational Model of Data for Large Shared Data Banks" for the prototype design. It was originally called *SEQUEL (Structured English QUEry Language)* that handled queries on the collection and organization of data - or simply known as a database. More features were added to the computer software to improve its performance, like building and managing database security, among others. When IBM researchers learned that there is another company that had the same "Sequel" trademark, they renamed it to "S-Q-L" (presently expanded as *Structured Query Language*).

Since it was first released to the public, SQL has already had many versions. In 1979, Relational Software, Incorporated (which later became the Oracle Corporation) released *ORACLE*, the first SQL product. Now, as the demand for computers that manage data has increased, the more SQL has become an industry standard in the field of Information Technology. Such formal standards are set and maintained by the *International Standards Organization*, or simply known as *ISO*. It was on 1986, based on IBM's implementation, that SQL has been recognized as the standard language in database communication. The following year, ISO accepted *ANSI SQL* as the international standard. ANSI stands for *American National Standards Institute*, which is an organization that approves certain standards in various US industries. Many revisions of the standards followed, such as in 1992 (SQL-92) and in 1999 (SQL-99). The latest one is now called SQL-2011, which was officially released in December 2011.

Uses of SQL

The corporate world is now shifting from merely producing products and providing services to investing in digital technologies that handle vast amounts of data, to be transformed to meaningful pieces of information that will generate more profitable income for the company. This is the primary objective of SQL – to access and manipulate data that will further lead to business insights. This flexible computer language has been the most widely used communication tool in handling databases (specifically relational databases that will be further discussed in Chapter 3 of this book).

Try to imagine that you are going to a foreign country for a vacation. You may need to learn that country's language to find your way around, as you explore the new place. When you try to ask someone for directions, who is local to that place and only speaks the country's language, then surely you will have a hard time understanding him. In this scenario, the foreign land will be your database in which you need to seek information, while SQL is the language that you will use to get what you need from the database.

From time to time, you will encounter the term *query*, which is also a part of the abbreviation of SQL. Query is basically the question written using an SQL statement that is being asked from the database. SQL then retrieves the needed information when any of the data in the database meets the requirements of the conditions of the given query. So, in real-life applications, such as an online store, when you execute your query for a specific item by entering your search criteria, SQL programming usually takes place in the background to manage the database connections. You are actually telling the database, through the help of SQL, what information you want to see and how you want it to be presented to you.

People Using SQL

SQL is not only applicable for IT professionals or geeks who possess remarkable programming skills. With the growing corporate world of today, non-IT personnel such as businessmen and managers, can also benefit from learning the semantics of SQL. This is because the computer language enables them to understand the ins and outs of their businesses using the data that drives every company. Moreover, it opens several career opportunities in the analytical, managerial, strategic or research fields - for those who want to step-up from their current positions. On the IT field, SQL knowledge can lead to more challenging roles such as database designers, administrators or scientists, systems engineers, project managers and software developers, among others.

In this chapter, you have learned an overview of SQL – its history, its primary purpose why it was created, and those who will profit from learning this powerful database software. In the next chapter, you will learn the essentials of database, which is the primary reason why SQL was designed in the first place.

Chapter Two: The Database Essentials

Before you start learning the technicalities of SQL as a computer language, this chapter will discuss first what a database is and its fundamental characteristics. You will also be informed why the business world is now driven to gather and manipulate data, to bring forth more profit.

Database Fundamentals

There are many ways to define or describe what a database is. In simple terms, it can be defined as a collection of items that can exist over a long period of time. Think of a calling card holder as a database that contains business cards with various information of people that you know (e.g. person's name, job title, company name, contact number). Another one is a printed telephone directory (more popularly known as the yellow pages) that contains the name, phone number and address of the registered residents living in a particular area.

Some define database more professionally, not just a collection of data. It is described as an organized tool, capable of keeping data or information, that you can retrieve in an effective and efficient way when the need arises. It can also be more strictly defined as a self-describing collection of objects that are integrated to one another. When you create representations of these physical or conceptual objects, then they will be called *records*. From the previous example of your calling card holder, if you wish to keep track of your business contacts then you have to assign each business card a specific record. Every record contains multiple information or data, such as an individual's name, job title, company name and address, phone number and more that you will now call the record's *attributes*.

A database does not only contain the data that you need, but also what you call its *metadata*. This is the information that defines or describes the data's structure within the given database (that is why it was defined earlier as a self-describing entity), stored in a region called *data dictionary*. Thus, data retrieval will be faster if you know how information is arranged and stored. Furthermore, relationships exist among the data items since they are integrated to one another. Check the following figure for a sample illustration of what a database is.

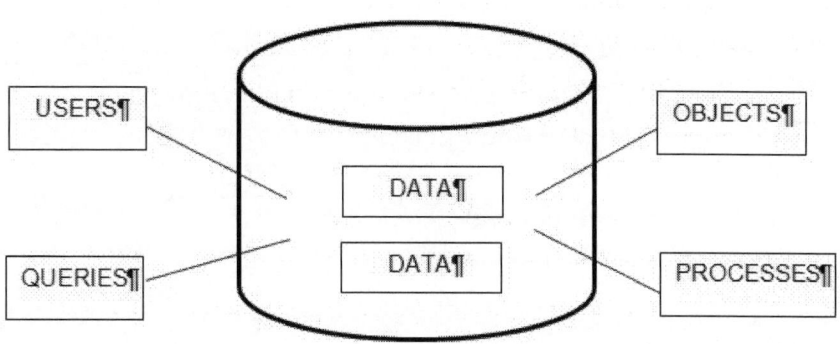

Whether a database contains a simple collection of a few records or a massive system composed of millions of records, it can be categorized into three types: personal, workgroup or departmental, and enterprise. Each category is characterized by the database size, the machinery size into which the database runs and how big the organization that manages it is.

- **Personal Database** – This is conceptualized and designed by a single person on a stand-alone computer. Its database structure is rather simple and the size is relatively small. For example, your personal electronic address book.

- **Workgroup/Departmental Database** – This is designed and created by individuals of a single workgroup or department within a certain organization. The database structure is larger and more complex, as compared to the personal category, which is also accessed by multiple users at the same time.

- **Enterprise Database** – Among the three categories, this type is conceptualized and created to handle the entire flow of information of very large organizations. Thus, the database design involves far more complex structures.

Relational Database Fundamentals

Taking the discussion further into a more technical aspect, a *relational database* is an entity consisting of logical units known as *tables*. This relational database model was first formulated by Dr. E. F. Codd in 1970. How the tables are related to each other defines their *relationships*. In this scenario, data is simplified into smaller yet more logical and manageable units that optimize the database performance. The following figure shows an illustration on how the various components of a relational database are connected to each other.

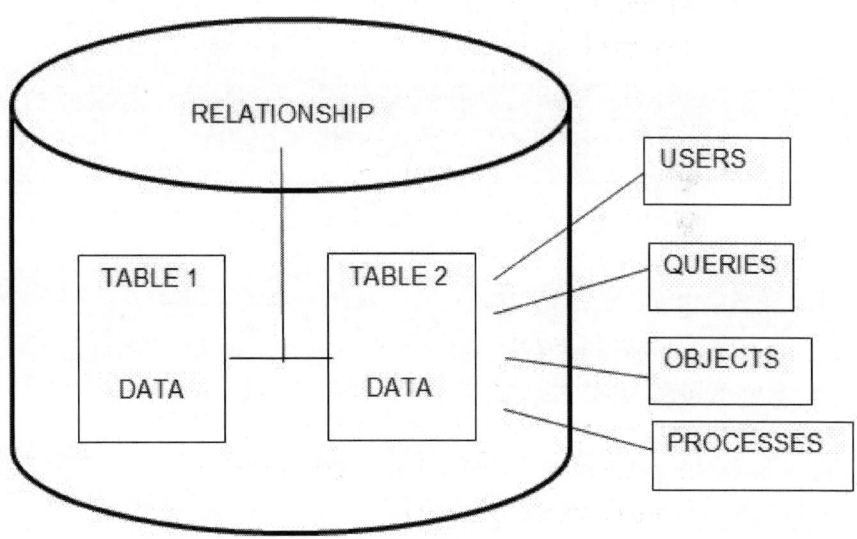

A table consists of rows and columns that store data. In a relational database, these tables are related to one another, improving the data retrieval process when a query is submitted by the user. For you to clearly picture out this idea, convert the information found on the calling card holder into a spreadsheet like a Microsoft Excel file. Assume that these are your contacts from companies that have ordered products and services from your business. You will have at least a CUSTOMER TABLE (containing all important information about your contacts) similar to the following:

CUSTOMER ID	NAME	POSITION	COMPANY	STATE	CONTACT NO
1	Kathy Ale	President	Tile Industrial	TX	3461234567
2	Kevin Lord	VP	Best Tooling	NY	5181234567
3	Kim Ash	Director	Car World	CA	5101234567
4	Abby Karr	Manager	West Mart	NV	7751234567

You will also have an ORDER TABLE that will store information such as order ID, date, quantity and more. Check the following table:

ORDER ID	ORDER DATE	CUSTOMER ID	PRODUCT ID	ORDER QTY
1	2016-05-23	1	4	300
2	2016-09-09	1	5	100
3	2016-02-17	3	2	150
4	2016-05-12	2	2	500

As you can see, each table looks like an array of rows and columns. Referring to the CUSTOMER TABLE, a row is also called a *record* or a *tuple* that holds information for a single customer. On the other hand, a column holds a single *attribute* of the customer (i.e., name, job title or position, company name and address, contact number). It is also self-consistent, meaning it contains the same type of data in every row. So, if a column contains the name of your customer in the first row, then the succeeding rows will have to show the names of your other customers. There is also no significance which row or column will appear first and which will be next, since there is no particular organization that is followed. Looking at both tables, you will notice that each one of them has a column that contains the same data value – CUSTOMER ID. This is now called the *common key*, which links the tables to one another in a relational database. The existence of the common keys makes it possible to merge data from multiple tables in forming a larger set of data entity.

The relation between the two tables consists of a two-dimensional array of data stored in rows and columns. The intersection of a row and a column is called a *cell*. Each cell contains single-valued entries and each row is unique. Thus, each cell has only one value and no duplicate rows. Going back to the CUSTOMER and ORDER TABLES, will be able to create the following relation by adding the CUSTOMER NAME that corresponds to the given CUSTOMER ID:

ORDER ID	CUSTOMER ID	CUSTOMER NAME
1	1	Kathy Ale
2	1	Kathy Ale
3	3	Kim Ash
4	2	Kevin Lord

You will see that there is no empty cell. One particular order referenced by the ORDER ID is associated to a particular customer, indicated by the CUSTOMER ID and CUSTOMER NAME. There are no two customers having the same ORDER ID. That is why, there will be no two rows that are exactly identical.

Database Management Systems

A database management system, or simply DBMS, is an important programming tool that consists of a set of programs that define, manage and process databases and all applications associated to them. Through this, you are able to build a structure and operate on the valuable data that the database holds, in a very efficient way. There are two main types of users that work on DBMS – the *conventional user* who retrieves or modifies data and the *administrator* who is responsible for maintaining the structure of the database.

The following are the key features of a DBMS:

- Allows the creation of new databases and their data structures
- Allows data query and modification using an appropriate programming language
- Allows the storage of vast amounts of data over a long period of time
- Enables database recovery in times of failure, error or intentional misuse
- Controls data access from many users at once

It was during the late 1960s when the first commercial DBMS appeared. It evolved from file systems that basically provided data storage for a certain period of time. Though such systems were capable of storing tremendous amount of data, computer professionals still have to face problems of data loss and an inefficient information retrieval system. There were also issues of control access, where errors occur when two users modify the same file at the same time. Some examples of these applications are airline reservation systems, banking systems and corporate record keeping systems, among others.

With the advancement of technology in the market today, you can find numerous programs that will be suitable for your DBMS requirements. There are applications that run on a small-scale level, like your personal computer or tablet. Some are built to run on large and powerful equipment, like those being used by multinational companies. Nevertheless, the on-going trend is for DBMS to be executed on multiple platforms or machines (whether large or small) that are interconnected to one another, forming an immense scalable network. IT experts have also found ways of how to store data using Internet technology in powerful data- centres, more popularly known as *clouds*. This cloud can be a public entity (managed by a large company like Microsoft or Google), or a private one, (maintained and stored via the intranet within an organization).

In this chapter, you have learned the essential features of a database and how it transforms to become a relational database. Also, you had an overview of the history and characteristics of database management systems. In the next chapter, you will learn the fundamental structure of the SQL language and its components.

Chapter Three: The SQL Structure

In this chapter, you will learn the fundamental features of the SQL language, and an overview of its programming aspect. In addition, you will be presented with a step-by-step instruction on where and how to download SQLite, a version of the SQL software that will be used all throughout the discussion of this e-Book.

SQL Fundamental Features

SQL is a flexible computer language that you can deploy in different ways to communicate with relational databases. This software has some distinct features that differentiates it from other programming applications. First and foremost, SQL is a nonprocedural language. Most computer programs (e.g., C, C++ and Java) solve problems by following a sequence of commands that is called a *procedure*. In this case, one specific operation is performed after another until the required task has been accomplished. The flow of operation can either be a linear sequence or a looping one, depending on what the programmer had specified. This is not the same for SQL. In using this application, you will just have to specify the output that you want, not how you want to generate the output. From the CUSTOMER TABLE, if you want to create a separate list of contacts whose companies are located in Texas, then you have to retrieve the rows where the STATE column contains "TX" as its value. In writing the SQL command, you don't have to indicate how the information should be retrieved. It is the primary role of the database management system to examine the database and decide how to generate the results you wanted.

Learning the SQL syntax is like understanding the English language structure. Its command language, comprised of a limited number of statements, performs three primary data functions - definition, manipulation and control. The SQL programming language also includes reserved words that are only to be used for specific purposes. Thus, you cannot use these words as names for variables, tables and columns; or in any other way apart from their intended use. Below are some of the most common reserved words in SQL:2011.

ABS	ALL	ALLOCATE	ALTER	AND	ANY
ARE	ARRAY	AS	AT	AVG	BEGIN
BETWEEN	BINARY	BOOLEAN	BOTH	BY	CALL
CASCADED	CASE	CEILING	CHAR	CHARACTER	CHECK
CLOSE	COLLATE	COLLECT	COLUMN	COMMIT	CONDITION
CONNECT	CONSTRAINT	CONVERT	COUNT	CREATE	CURSOR
CYCLE	DATE	DAY	DEALLOCATE	DEC	DECIMAL
DECLARE	DEFAULT	DELETE	DESCRIBE	DISCONNECT	DISTINCT
DOUBLE	DROP	DYNAMIC	EACH	ELEMENT	ELSE
END	ESCAPE	EVERY	EXCEPT	EXECUTE	EXISTS
EXTERNAL	EXTRACT	FALSE	FETCH	FILTER	FLOAT
FLOOR	FOR	FOREVER	FREE	FROM	FULL
FUNCTION	FUSION	GET	GLOBAL	GRANT	GROUP
GROUPING	HAVING	HOLD	HOUR	HOURS	IDENTITY
IN	INNER	INOUT	INSERT	INT	INTEGER
INTERSECT	INTERVAL	INTO	IS	JOIN	KEEP
LANGUAGE	LARGE	LEAD	LEFT	LIKE	LOCAL
LOWER	MATCH	MAX	MEMBER	MERGE	METHOD
MINUTE	MOD	MODULE	MONTH	MULTISET	NATIONAL
NATURAL	NEW	NIL	NO	NONE	NORMALIZ

					E
NOT	NULL	NUMERIC	OF	OFFSET	OLD
ON	ONLY	OPEN	OR	ORDER	OUT
OVER	OVERLAY	PARAMETER	PARTITION	POSITION	POWER
PRECISION	PREPARE	PRIMARY	PROCEDURE	RANGE	RANK
REAL	RECURSIVE	REF	REFERENCES	REFERENCING	RELEASE
RESULT	RETURN	REVOKE	RIGHT	ROLLBACK	ROLLUP
ROW	ROWS	SCOPE	SCROLL	SEARCH	SECOND
SELECT	SET	SIMILAR	SOME	SPECIFIC	SQL
START	STATIC	SUM	SYMMETRIC	SYSTEM	TABLE
THEN	TIME	TIMESTAMP	TO	TRANSLATE	TREAT
TRIGGER	TRUNCATE	TRIM	TRUE	UNION	UNIQUE
UNKNOWN	UPDATE	UPPER	USER	USING	VALUE
VALUES	VARCHAR	VARYING	VERSION	WHEN	WHENEVER
WHERE	WINDOW	WITH	WITHIN	WITHOUT	YEAR

If you think that an SQL database is just a collection of tables, then you are wrong. There are additional structures that need to be specified to maintain the integrity of your data, such as schemas, domains and constraints.

- **Schema** – This is also called the *conceptual view* or the *complete logical view* that defines the entire database structure and provides overall table organization. Such schema is considered a metadata – stored in tables and part of the database (just like tables that consist of regular data).

- **Domain** – This specifies the set of all finite data values you can store in a particular table column or attribute. For example, in our previous CUSTOMER TABLE, the STATE column can only contain the values "TX", "NY", "CA" and "NV" if you only provide products and services in the states of Texas, New York, California and Nevada respectively. So, these four state abbreviations are the domain of the STATE attribute.

- **Constraint** – Often ignored but one of the important database components, this sets down the rules that identify what data values a specific table attribute can contain. Incorporating tight constraints assures that database users only enter valid data into a particular column. Together with defined table characteristics, column constraints determine its domain. Using the same STATE column as an example with the given constraint of only the four values, if a database user enters "NJ" for New Jersey, then the entry will not be accepted. The system will not proceed until a valid value is entered for the STATE attribute, unless the database structure needs to be updated due to sudden business changes.

SQL Command Types

Before you start programming in SQL, you need to understand its basic command categories in performing various functions – database creation, object manipulation, data population and update, data deletion, query submission, access control and database administration, among others. The following are the main categories:

- **Data Definition Language (DDL)**

    Data Definition Language (or simply DDL) enables you to create, change or restructure, and even destroy the basic elements that are contained in a relational database. DDL focuses only on the structure, not the data contained within the elements. These basic elements or data objects include tables, schemas, views and more. Having no independent physical existence, a *view* is regarded as a virtual table in which its definition only exists in the metadata. However, the view's data comes from the table (or tables) where you will derive the view. Stated below are some of the most common DDL commands:

    - **CREATE** – This command statement is responsible for building the database structure. Its syntax is:

CREATE TABLE
CREATE VIEW

- **ALTER** – This command statement is in charge of changing the database structure after it has been created. Its syntax is:

  ALTER TABLE
  ALTER VIEW

- **DROP** – This command is the reverse of the CREATE statement, which destroys the database structure. Its syntax is:

  DROP TABLE
  DROP VIEW

- **Data Manipulation Language (DML)**

Data Manipulation Language (or simply DML) consists of SQL commands that handle data maintenance functions. This means that you are able to manipulate the data contained within the relational database objects. The command statements, which read like normal English sentences, will allow you to enter, change, remove or retrieve data. The following are the DML statements commonly used:

  - **INSERT** – This command statement is used to insert new data values into a certain table. To add values into a table with two columns, use the following syntax:

    INSERT INTO *TABLE_NAME*
    VALUES ('value1', 'value2');

    TABLE_NAME is the name of the table where you will be adding the new values. The number of items inside the *VALUES* parenthesis represents the number of columns of the table, which are arranged in the same order as the said columns. If the values are of character or date/time data types, they need to be enclosed by single quotation marks. This is not required for numeric or null values (the null value should be written as NULL).

- **UPDATE** – This command statement is used to modify or alter pre-existing data values in a table, not add or remove records. The update is done one table at a time or multiple rows/columns of one table within a database. To change a single column, use the following syntax:

> UPDATE *TABLE_NAME*
> SET *COLUMN_NAME* = 'value'
> [WHERE *CONDITION*];

As long as the given WHERE clause is satisfied, then the value of the *COLUMN_NAME* will be updated. This could be within one or multiple records of the given *TABLE_NAME*.

- **DELETE** – This command statement deletes certain records or even the entire table, not data values from specific columns. To remove a single row or multiple records from a table, use the following syntax:

DELETE FROM *TABLE_NAME*
[WHERE *CONDITION*];

The WHERE clause is an important part of this command if you want to delete selected rows from the *TABLE_NAME*.

- **Data Query Language (DQL)**

Data Query Language (or simply DQL) consists of commands that perform data selection, which is the main focus of relational database users in the world of SQL. The statement used is SELECT that can be accompanied by other clauses or options so that your extracted results will be in an organized and readable format. You can submit a query to the database using a separate application interface or just a single command-line. The following is a syntax for a simple SELECT statement:

SELECT [* | ALL | DISTINCT *COLUMN1, COLUMN2*]
FROM *TABLE1* [, *TABLE2*];

Using the asterisk (*) means that all columns of the given table are included in the output and will be displayed. The ALL option extracts and displays all values, even duplicates, for a column. On the other hand, using the keyword DISTINCT prevents duplicate rows from being included and displayed in the output. What follows the FROM keyword is a list of one or more tables where you want to get the data. The columns and tables specified in the syntax are all separated by commas.

- **Data Control Language (DCL)**

    Data Control Language (or simply DCL) consists of commands that allow you to manage data access within the database. Furthermore, the database is protected from accidental or intentional misuse by controlling user privileges. DCL concentrates on transactions, which capture all SQL statements that perform database operations and save them in a log file. The following are the common DCL command statements:

    - **GRANT** – This statement provides you with certain privileges, like giving you the permission to access the database. Its syntax is:

        GRANT *PRIVILEGE1, PRIVILEGE2, ...* TO *USER_NAME*

    - **REVOKE** – This statement revokes your privileges, like removing your permission to access the database. Its syntax is:

        REVOKE *PRIVILEGE1, PRIVILEGE2, ...* TO *USER_NAME*

- **Transactional Control Commands**

    Transactional control commands allow users to manipulate various transactions in maintaining database integrity. In SQL, transactions begin when applications are executed. The very first transaction is started at the onset of the SQL application, while the last transaction is ended when the application is terminated. The following are the common transactional control commands:

    o **COMMIT** – This statement completes a transaction by making the changes you made to the database permanent, or simply saving the transactions. Its syntax is:

    COMMIT [WORK];

    In the previous command line, the keyword **WORK** is optional.

    o **ROLLBACK** – This statement's primary function is to restore the database system to its previous state or undo all the actions that took place in the transaction log. Its syntax is:

ROLLBACK [WORK];

In the previous command line, the keyword **WORK** is optional.

- **SAVEPOINT** – This statement works with the ROLLBACK command, wherein it creates sections or points within groups of transactions in which you will be performing the ROLLBACK command. Its syntax is:

SAVEPOINT *SAVEPOINT_NAME*;

SQLite Installation Instructions and Database Features

Before you start overwhelming yourself with various database solutions and SQL command lines, you need to determine first your purpose; why you are creating a database. This will further determine other database design considerations such as size, complexity, type of machine where the application will run, storage medium, and more. When you start thinking of your database requirements, you need to know up to what level of detail should be considered in your design. Too much detail will result to a very complex design that further wastes time and effort, and even your computer's storage space. Too little will lead to a poor performing, corrupt and worthless database. Once you are done with the design phase, then you can decide which database software you can download to start your SQL experience.

For the sake of this e-Book's discussion, SQLite, a simple software library, will be used as a starter database engine to design, build and deploy applications. A free and stand-alone database software that is quick to download and easy to administer, SQLite was developed by Richard Hipp and his team of programmers. It was designed so that it can be easily configured and implemented, which does not require any client-server setup at all. Thus, SQLite is considered one of the most widely used database software applications in the world.

Stated below are some of the major features of SQLite:

- Transactions are atomic, consistent, isolated and durable
- Compilation is simple and easy
- System crashes and power failures are supported
- Full SQL implementation with a stand-alone command-line interface client
- Code footprint is significantly small
- Adaptable and adjustable to larger projects
- Self-contained with no external dependencies
- Portable and supports other platforms like Windows, Android, iOS, Mac, Solaris and more

In using SQLite, you need to download *SQLiteStudio* as your database manager and editor. With its intuitive interface, this software is very light yet fast and powerful. You don't even need to install it, just download, unpack and run the application. Follow these simple steps in downloading SQLiteStudio on a Windows 10 computer:

1. Go to http://sqlitestudio.pl/?act=about. You should get the following page:

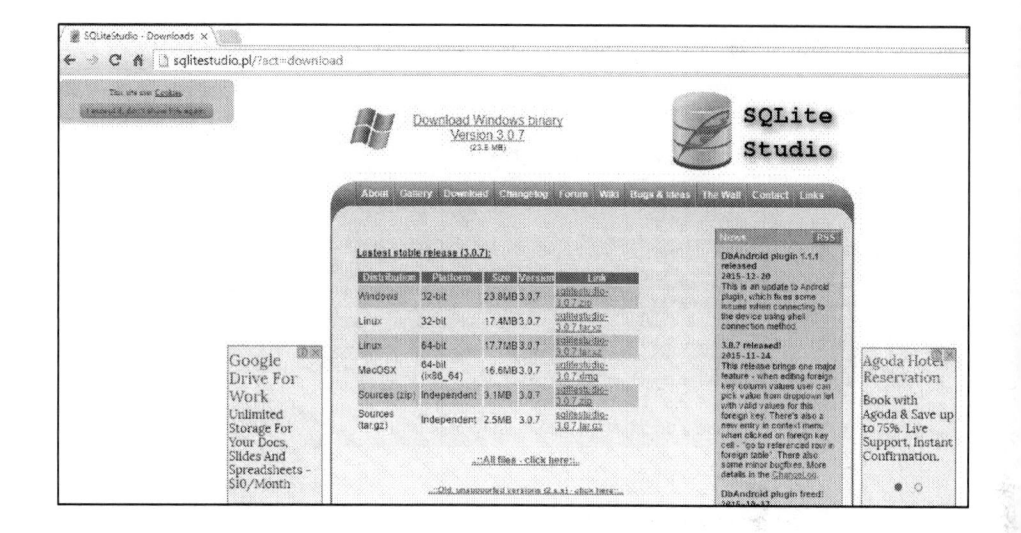

2. Check the version of your computer's operating system then click the appropriate link to start downloading the software.

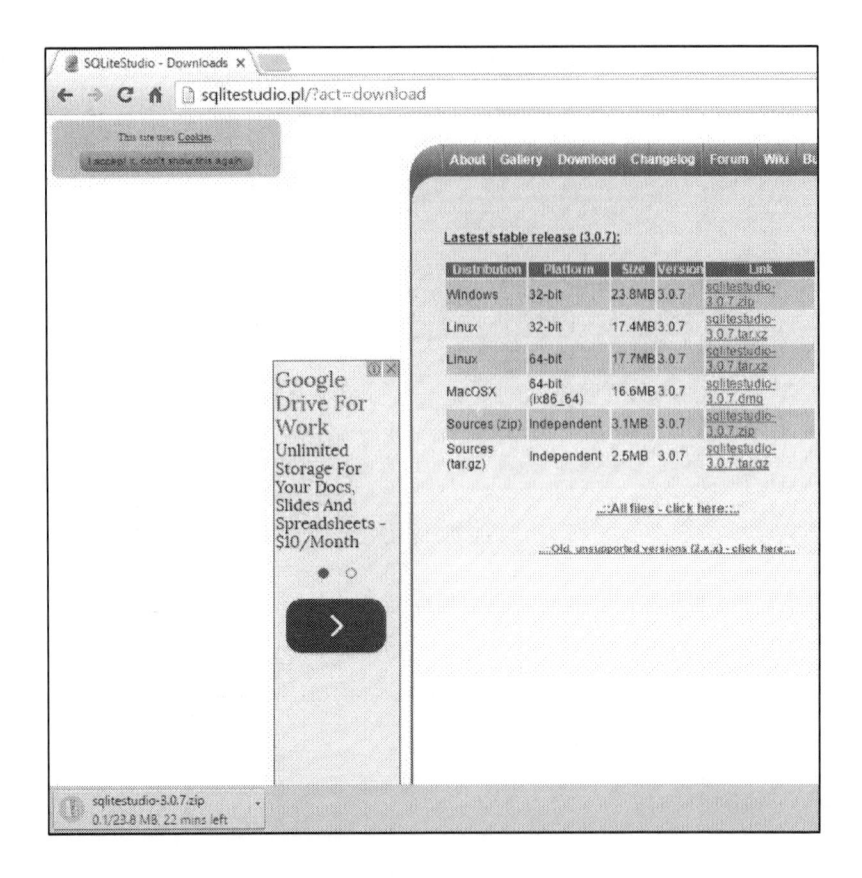

3. After downloading the software, go to the folder where the application was saved (usually the Downloads Folder in Windows). Click on the *Extract* tab on top then choose the *Extract all* option.

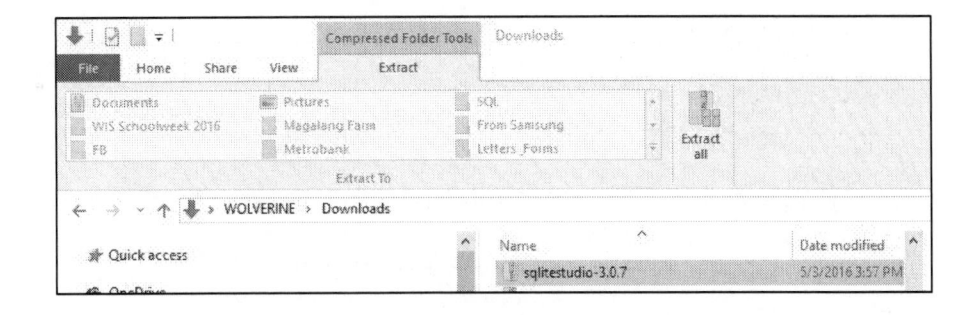

4. You will get the *Extract Compressed (Zipped) Folders* dialog box. Change the destination folder to C:\SQL then click the *Extract* button. This will be the folder where all your SQLite files will be saved.

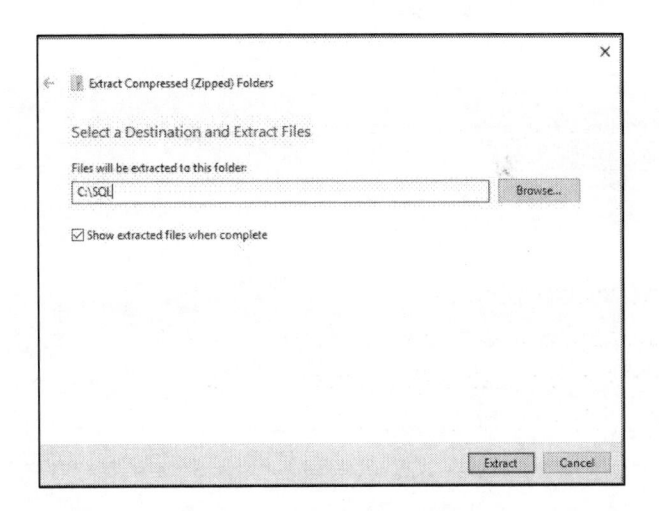

5. Once all the files have been extracted, you will have the SQLiteStudio subfolder.

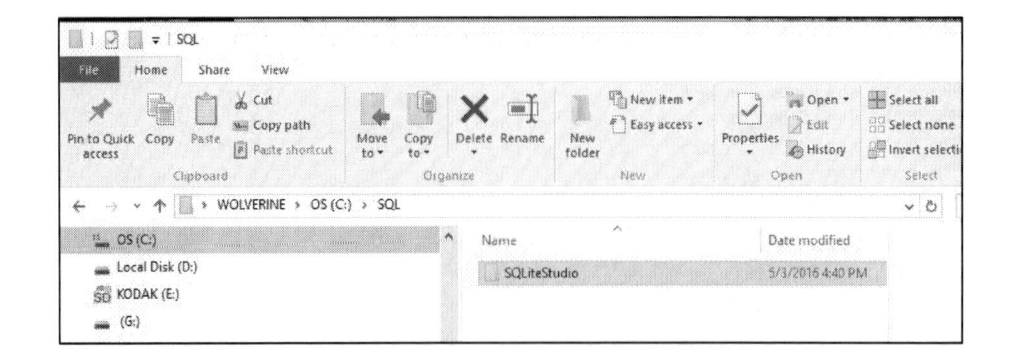

6. Find the application program named SQLiteStudio inside the subfolder. To create a shortcut on your desktop (so you can quickly launch the application), right-click the filename, select *Send to* option then choose *Desktop (create shortcut)*.

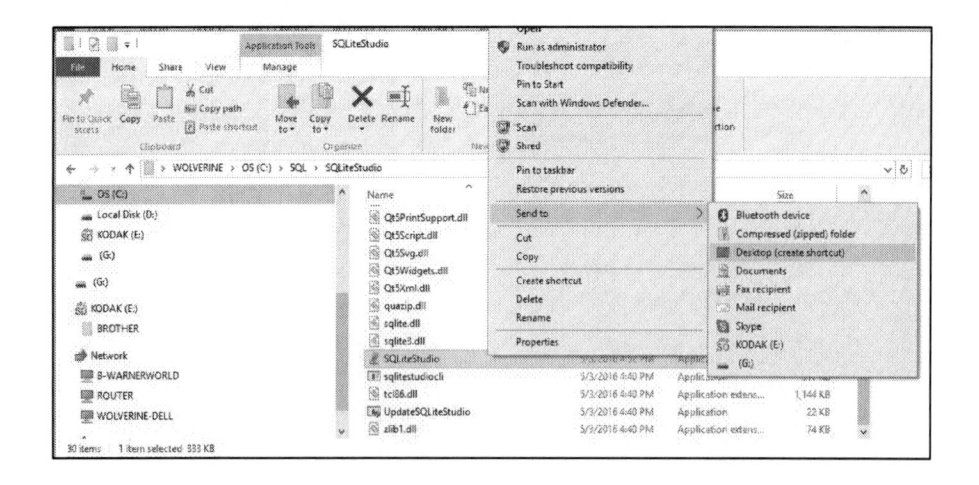

40

7. When you double-click the SQLiteStudio icon on your desktop,

8. you should get the following screen:

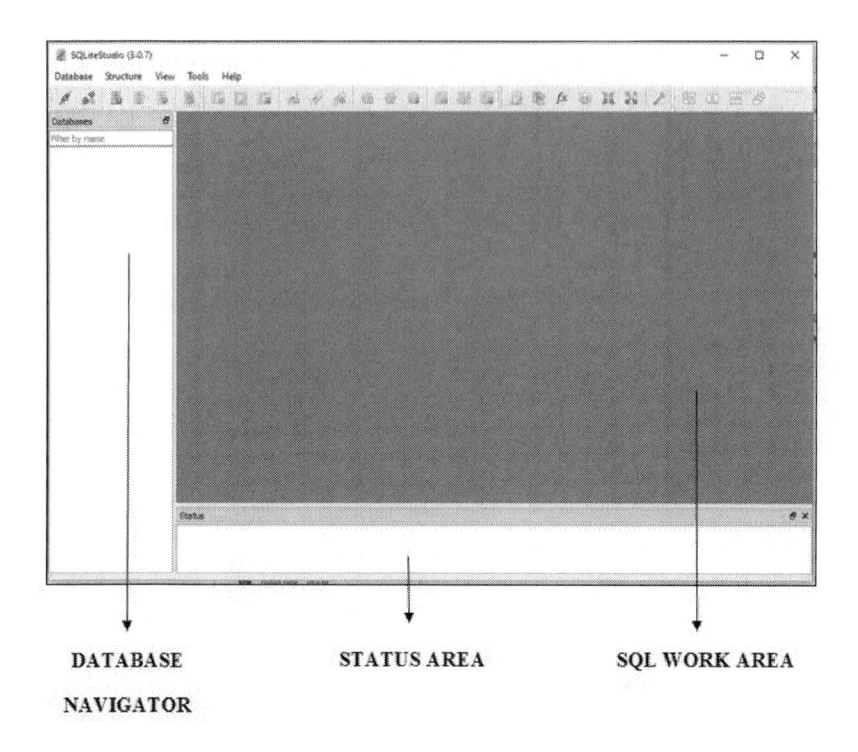

DATABASE NAVIGATOR   **STATUS AREA**   **SQL WORK AREA**

The *Database Navigator* (left pane) shows all the logical units of the database such as tables and views. The gray pane at the right is the *SQL Work Area* where you will write your query statements. You will have a better understanding of this program's graphical user interface in the succeeding chapters.

In this chapter, you have learned the fundamental features of the SQL database language, which includes program flow, syntax characteristic, reserved words list, schema, domain, constraint and more. The main categories of SQL commands were also introduced, that govern the various functions of the programming language. You were also given a guide on how to download and install SQLite and SQLiteStudio for your application software. In the next chapter, you will learn the definition of data and its various types supported by the different SQL implementations.

Chapter Four: Data Types

In this chapter, you will learn what data is, its characteristics, and the various types that the SQL programming language supports. There are different general types of data that are further categorized into several subtypes. However, it is advisable that you use defined data types to ensure the portability and comprehensibility of your database.

Definition of Data

Since a database is a collection of information, it can store names, numbers, images, calculations, financial amounts, characters and so on. This stored information is what you call *data*, which you can change or manipulate anytime you want. When you start providing rules on how you write and store data, then you are dealing with *data types*. Data types take into consideration the length allocated by the database for every column in the table, and what values it could contain - whether it is alphanumeric, just numbers, graphics, date or time. By defining what data is stored in each database field, you are preventing the occurrence of data entry errors. This form of validation that controls incorrect data to be entered into the database is also called *field definition*.

Each database field will have a specific value if it contains a data item. There are times, however, that a certain field does not have any data item at all. In this case, the field's value is considered *null* - meaning the value is not known. This null value is different from the numeric zero value or the blank character value, since zeroes and blanks are definite values. The following are scenarios when you may have a null value:

- You don't know what the value is yet even if it possibly exists.
- The value does not exist yet.
- The value is out of range.
- The field is not applicable for a particular row.

Types of Data

The following are the general data types predefined in the SQL language (that are further categorized into subtypes):

- **Numeric** – The value defined by the numeric data type is some kind of a number, which could either be expressed with an exact, or just an approximate, value.

    o **Exact Numeric**

- **INTEGER** – This consists only of whole numbers that are both positive and negative. It does not contain a decimal nor a fractional part. The value ranges from -2,147,483,648 to 2,147,483,647, with an allocated 4 bytes of storage size.

- **SMALLINT** – This is used in replacement of integers to save storage space, but with a precision that cannot be larger than that of an integer. Precision in computer programming is the maximum total of significant digits a number can have. The value ranges from -32,768 to +32,767, with an allocated 2 bytes of storage size.

- **BIGINT** – This is the reverse of the SMALLINT, where its minimum precision is the same as the INTEGER data type or greater. The value ranges from -9,223,372,036,854,775,808 to 9,223,372,036,854,775,807, with an allocated 8 bytes of storage size.

- **NUMERIC (p, s)** – In addition to the integer part, this data type also contains a fractional component that indicates the precision and scale of the value. Scale is the number of digits or places reserved in a fractional part of the data, located at the right side of the decimal point. In NUMERIC (p, s), 'p' specifies the precision while 's' is for the scale. For example, NUMERIC (6, 3) means that the number's absolute value will only be up to 999.999 (6 total significant digits with 3 digits following the decimal point).

- **DECIMAL (p, s)** – Like the NUMERIC data type, this has a fractional component where you can specify both the value precision and scale. However, this data type allows greater precision. For example, DECIMAL (6, 3) can contain values up to 999.999 but the database will still accept values larger than 999.999. Let's say you entered the number 123.4564, this will be rounded off to 123.456. The allocated storage size for this data type is based on the given precision.

47

- Approximate Numeric

  - **REAL (s)** – This consists of a single-precision, floating-point number where the decimal point can "float" to different places in the said number. This means that this data type's decimal value has a limitless precision and a scale of variable lengths. For example, the values for π (pi) can include 3.14159, 3.14 and 3.1 (each value has its own precision). For single-precision, floating point numbers, their precision is between 1 and 21 inclusive. It also allocates 4 bytes of storage size for its values.

  - **DOUBLE PRECISION (p, s)** – This consists of a double-precision, floating-point number and the capacity is twice of the REAL data type. This data type comes in handy when you require more precise numbers, like in most scientific fields of discipline. For double-precision, floating point numbers, their precision is between 22 and 53 inclusive. It also allocates 8 bytes of storage size for its values.

- **FLOAT (p, s)** – This is the data type that allows you to specify the precision and lets the computer decide whether you will go for a single- or a double-precision. It actually pertains to both REAL and DOUBLE PRECISION, depending on the precision you have specified. Because of this characteristic, it is easier to move the database from one computer platform to another.

- **String** – The string data type stores alphanumeric information and is also considered one of the most commonly used data types.

  o **CHARACTER (n) or CHAR (n)** – This data type is also known as a fixed-length string or a constant character. This means that all the strings stored in that particular column have the same length, which is represented by 'n' (the number of characters or the maximum allocated length for the defined field). For example, if you set the column's data type to CHAR (23) then the maximum length of any data entered in the field is 23 characters. If the string's length is less than 23, then SQL fills the remaining spaces with blanks. This is the drawback of using fixed-length strings because storage space is wasted. On the other hand, if there is no value provided for 'n', then SQL assumes a length of one character. The maximum length for the CHARACTER data type is 254.

- **CHARACTER VARYING (n) or VARCHAR (n)** – This is used when the data entries are of different lengths, or not constant, but you don't want SQL to fill the remaining spaces with blanks. Thus, the exact number of characters you enter will be stored in the database - further saving storage space. This data type has no default value and its maximum length is 32,672 characters.

- **CHARACTER LARGE OBJECT (CLOB)** – Introduced in SQL:1999, this variable-length data type is used to contain unicode character-based information that is too big to be stored as a CHARACTER type, such as large documents. The maximum value of a CLOB is up to 2,147,483,647 characters long.

- **Date and Time** – This data type manages any information concerning dates and times.

    o **DATE** – This data type provides storage for the year, month and day values of a date, in that particular order. The year value is expressed using four digits, which can be represented by any value ranging from 0001 up to 9999. As for the month and day values, they are both expressed using two digits. The format for the date data type is yyyy-mm-dd.

    o **TIME** – This data type stores and displays time values with an hour-minute-second format ("HH:MM:SS").

    o **DATETIME** – When the value contains both date and time information then you use the DATETIME data type, which is displayed using the "YYYY-MM-DD HH:MM:SS" format. The valid range of values for this type is from "1000-01-01 00:00:00" to "9999-12-31 23:59:59".

- o **TIMESTAMP** – This is similar to the DATETIME data type but the range of values is from "1970-01-01 00:00:01" UTC to "2038-01-19 03:14:07" UTC.

- **Boolean** – This data type consists of values that are used for data comparison: TRUE, FALSE, or NULL. For data to be returned, all the conditions of the specified criteria for a given query should be met – meaning the Boolean value is TRUE. If data is not returned, then the value is either FALSE or NULL.

User-Defined Data Type

After learning the general pre-defined data types, you will now move to user-defined data types or simply UDTs. By the name itself, these are the data values that the user defines or specifies based on the existing data types. Thus, customization is allowed to maximize storage space and meet other user requirements. Furthermore, database application development becomes more flexible for programmers. This means that you can use UDTs when you need to enter the same type of data in a column that will be defined in several tables. To define UDTs, you can use the CREATE TYPE statement.

For example, if you want to define and differentiate USDollar and UKPound as two currencies for your database then create the following UDTS:

CREATE TYPE USDollar AS DECIMAL (9, 2) ;

CREATE TYPE UKPound AS DECIMAL (9, 2) ;

Even if both data types were created using the predefined DECIMAL type, each has its own function and characteristic in the database. Going back to the sample customer and order information from the previous chapters, you can now create the following invoice tables that include the two UDTs:

```
CREATE TABLE AmericaInvoice (
    InvoiceID    INTEGER         PRIMARY KEY,
    CustomerID   INTEGER,
    OrderID      INTEGER,
    TotalSaleAmt USDollar,
    ShippingFee  USDollar
) ;


CREATE TABLE UnitedKingdomInvoice (
    InvoiceID    INTEGER         PRIMARY KEY,
    CustomerID   INTEGER,
    OrderID      INTEGER,
    TotalSaleAmt USDollar,
    ShippingFee  USDollar
```

    );

In this chapter, you have learned the characteristics of the various data types available in the SQL language. You were also able to understand the need to create user-defined data types to make your database less complicated and more portable. In the next chapter, you will learn how to use the different Data Definition Language statements in creating database objects using SQLiteStudio.

Chapter Five: Data Definition Language Statements

In this chapter, you will gain a deeper understanding of the three Data Definition Language statements – CREATE, ALTER and DROP. Using SQLiteStudio, you will also learn how to encode the corresponding SQL statements that handle the database structure.

Again, a database object is any defined logical unit that stores or references data. When you have a collection of database objects, you create a *schema* that is associated with one particular database owner. The focus of this chapter is the basic form of data storage, which is the relational database table. A simple table further consists of rows, which corresponds to the records of data, and columns, which are also known as fields that contain an assigned particular type of data. A database table will always have at least one column and a row that is composed of one or more fields.

CREATE Statement

The numerous forms of the SQL CREATE statement are responsible for constructing vital database structures and objects – tables, views, schemas, domains and so on. The act of creating tables could be easy, but you need to take into consideration numerous factors. Planning table structures before actual implementation could save you time and effort since you do not need to reconfigure after the tables have been created.

Here are some of the factors to take into consideration when creating tables:

- Type of data the table will contain
- Table and column names
- Primary key (the column that makes each row of data unique to avoid duplicate records in a table)
- Column length
- Columns containing null values

Syntax:

CREATE TABLE *TABLE_NAME*
(field1   *DATA_TYPE* [not null],
 field2   *DATA_TYPE* [not null],
 field3   *DATA_TYPE* [not null],
 field4   *DATA_TYPE* [not null],
 field5   *DATA_TYPE* [not null]);

The column names (field1, field2, field3, field4 and field5) and the field data types are written inside the parenthesis, separated by commas. Anything indicated inside the brackets are considered optional and the syntax statement finally ends with a semicolon.

Using the CUSTOMER TABLE from Chapter 2, you will create a new database table using SQLiteStudio.

- **Create a New Database**

    1. Open SQLiteStudio by double-clicking the application icon on your desktop.

    2. Click the DATABASE menu then select ADD A DATABASE.

    3. Type **Sample_DB** inside the FILE input box (which is the name of the new database) then click OK.

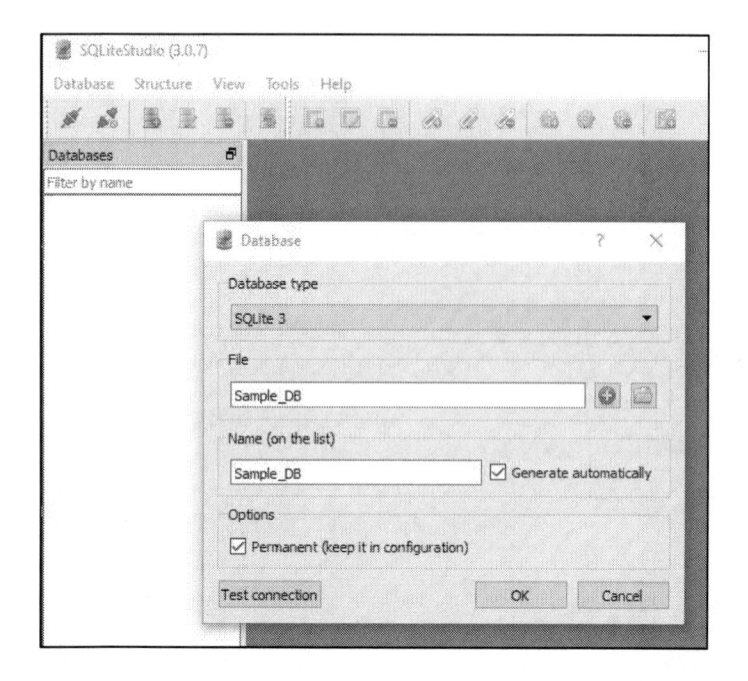

4. You will now have the **Sample_DB** object inside the Database Navigator pane.

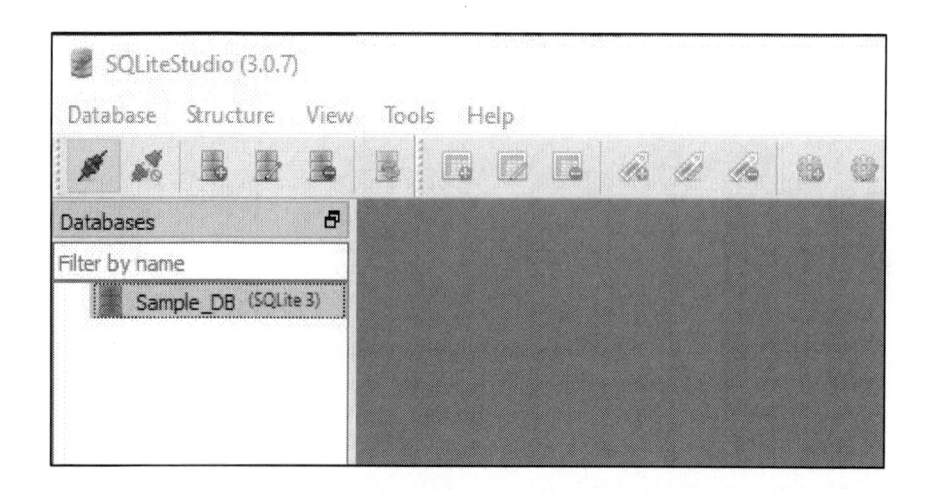

- **Create a New Table**

    1. Click the TOOLS menu then select OPEN SQL EDITOR. You will have the SQL editor area at the right pane. If you double-click **Sample_DB**, you will see TABLES and VIEWS under the database object. Right now, there are no tables nor views present so you will create one using the SQL Editor pane.

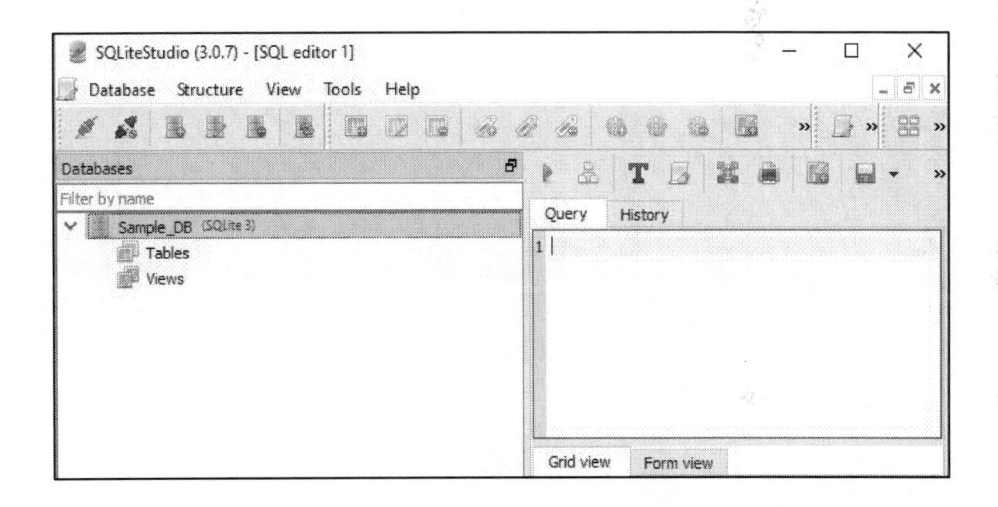

    2. Under the QUERY Tab, type the following lines of code

        CREATE TABLE Customer_TBL
        (CustomerID INTEGER NOT NULL PRIMARY KEY,
        CustomerName VARCHAR NOT NULL,

JobPosition VARCHAR,
CompanyName VARCHAR NOT NULL,
USState VARCHAR NOT NULL,
ContactNo BIGINTEGER NOT NULL);

```
1  CREATE TABLE Customer_TBL
2  (CustomerID INTEGER NOT NULL PRIMARY KEY,
3      CustomerName VARCHAR NOT NULL,
4      JobPosition VARCHAR,
5      CompanyName VARCHAR NOT NULL,
6      USState VARCHAR NOT NULL,
7      ContactNo BIGINTEGER NOT NULL);
```

3. Click the EXECUTE QUERY button on top of the QUERY Tab or press F9 on the keyboard. You will now have the **Customer_TBL** table with 6 columns.

ALTER Statement

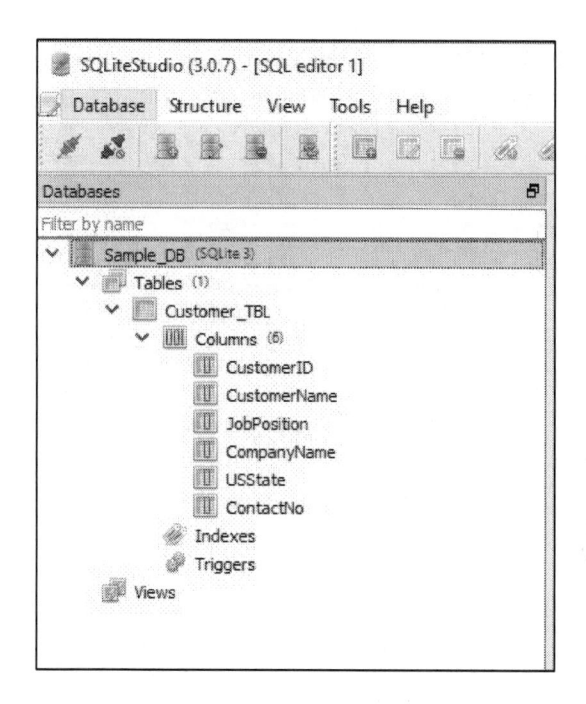

The SQL ALTER statement is used to modify database objects, specifically tables. Altering table elements can include adding and dropping columns, changing column definitions, adding and dropping constraints, modifying table storage values and more.

Syntax:

ALTER TABLE *TABLE_NAME* [modify] [column *COLUMN_NAME*]
  [*DATA TYPE* | null not null]

[restrict | cascade]
[drop] [constraint *CONSTRAINT_NAME*]
[add] [column] *COLUMN DEFINITION*;

- **Alter a Table by Adding a New Column**

1. A new column that contains the company address of the customer will be added to the **Customer_TBL** table. Type the following lines of code under the QUERY tab:

    ALTER TABLE Customer_TBL ADD
    CompanyAdd VARCHAR;

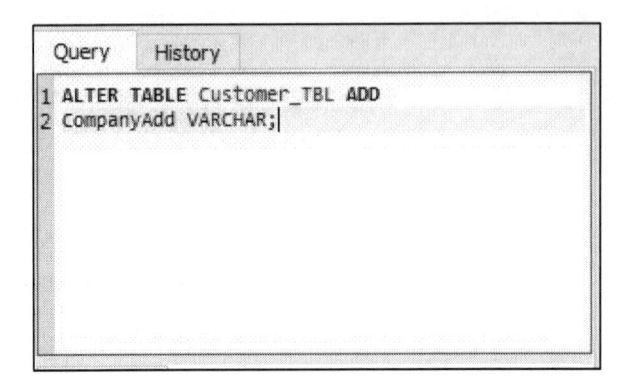

```
Query   History
1 ALTER TABLE Customer_TBL ADD
2 CompanyAdd VARCHAR;|
```

2. After clicking the EXECUTE QUERY button, the **CompanyAdd** column is added after the **ContactNo** column. This field contains values of string data type.

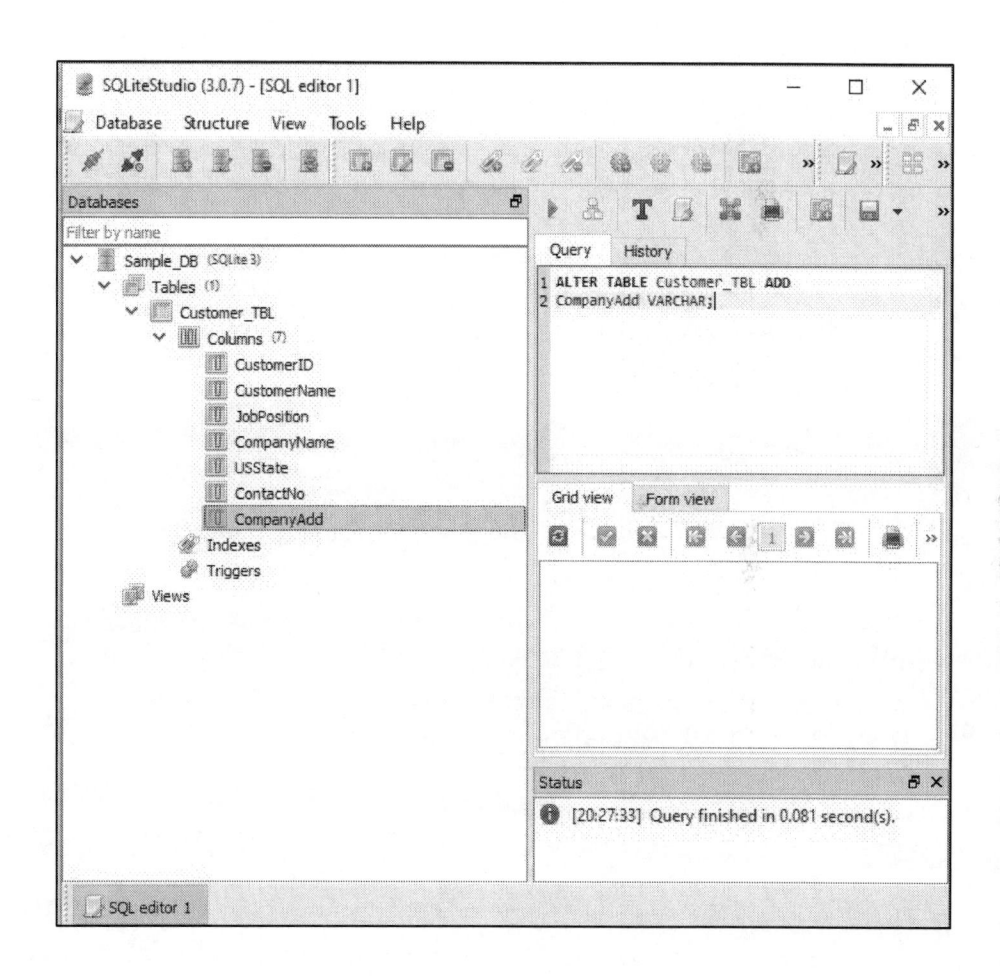

DROP Statement

You use the SQL DROP statement if you want to delete database objects. Thus, the DROP TABLE statement is used to delete tables that you do not need anymore. Once this line is executed, all the data and metadata contained in the table are also removed. DROP TABLE is considered to be the easiest command to execute. However, an error will occur if the table to be deleted is being referenced by another table in the database. That is why you need to be cautious when performing the DROP statement to avoid deleting objects by mistake (most especially if there are multiple users who access the database).

Syntax:

DROP TABLE *TABLE_NAME* [restrict | cascade]

The RESTRICT option is used if an error is to be returned when a table referenced by another database object is dropped. On the other hand, the CASCADE option allows the table and all other referencing objects to be deleted. There are some SQL application programs that do not permit the CASCADE option to guarantee that there will be no invalid database objects.

- **Drop an Existing Table**

    1. Since there is only one table in the database (**Customer_TBL**), you do not need to worry whether

to use the RESTRICT or the CASCADE option. Simply enter the following line of code inside the QUERY tab.

DROP TABLE Customer_TBL;

```
Query   History
1 DROP TABLE Customer_TBL;
```

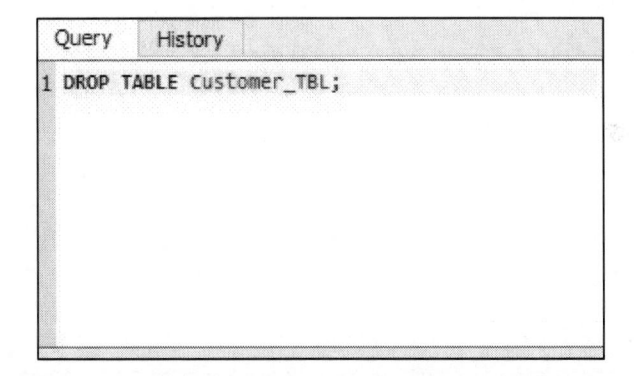

2. Click the EXECUTE QUERY button and instantly the **Customer_TBL** table is deleted.

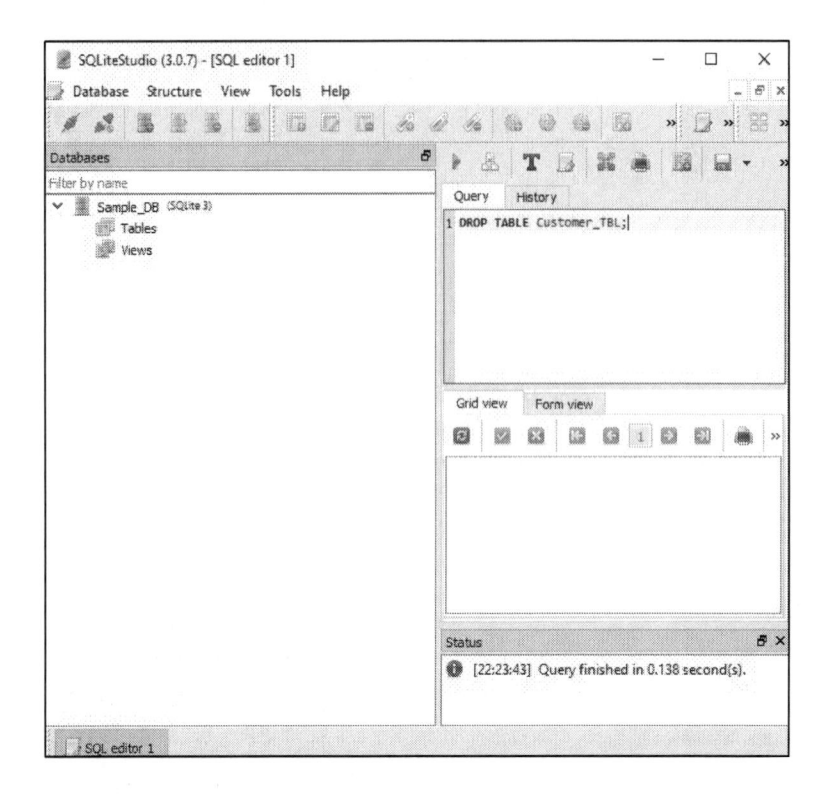

In this chapter, you have learned how to encode programming lines using the common DDL command statements in creating, altering and dropping database tables in SQL. In the next chapter, you will learn the different DML commands that will allow you to manipulate information contained in database tables.

Chapter Six: Data Manipulation Language Statements

In this chapter, you will learn how to manipulate database tables and make them useful through data insertion, deletion and update. To accomplish this, you will be programming in SQLiteStudio using three Data Manipulation Language statements – INSERT, DELETE and DROP.

Normally, such tables are empty after they have been created. The data that you can store in your database objects can be in various formats – non-digital, semi-digital and fully digital. Non-digital format means that the data needs to be extracted from a non-electronic source, like customer information from business cards. In this case, you are required to store the data manually into your database. As for the semi-digital, the data could already be in some sort of digital form but not the same format as your database tables. For example, you could have records of your customers' business cards stored in a Microsoft Excel file that you may need to translate into an appropriate format fit for your database. Lastly, fully digital means that all of your customer information is already in electronic format that also matches the layout of your database.

The current data format will further determine how you will be able to manipulate your database. This is where the DML commands become useful in entering new data, updating existing data and deleting data from tables.

INSERT Statement

The process of entering new data could be done either manually through individual commands, or automatically using batch process programs. There are also factors that will determine what and how much data you can insert into your database tables – field length, column data type, table size and more. In populating tables with data, you will use the INSERT statement.

- **One Row at a Time**

    When you want to enter all the data into a single row of your database table, you can create a form-based data entry application. In this feature, a screen is designed that contains fields where you can input the information being asked - for every column in the table. Use the following syntax in adding data one row at a time:

    INSERT INTO *TABLE_NAME* [(column_1, column_2, ... , column_n)]
    VALUES (value_1, value_2, ..., value_n) ;

Anything inside the square brackets are considered optional, meaning you don't need to list the column names. By the way, "n" is the maximum number of table columns. The default order of the column list is the same order as your column tables. Thus, if you list the items inside the VALUES section in the same order as your table columns, then the values will be entered in the correct columns. You only need to indicate the column names if you need to specify the values in a different order.

Now, let us insert records to our Customer_TBL table using the customer information provided in the Chapter 2.

1. Type the following programming lines in the SQL editor:

INSERT INTO Customer_TBL (CustomerID, CustomerName, JobPosition,
    CompanyName, USState, ContactNo)
VALUES (1, 'Kathy Ale', 'President', 'Tile Industrial', 'TX', 3461234567)

```
Query   History
1 INSERT INTO Customer_TBL (CustomerID, CustomerName, JobPosition, CompanyName, USState, ContactNo)
2 VALUES (1, 'Kathy Ale', 'President', 'Tile Industrial', 'TX', 3461234567)
```

2. Click the EXECUTE QUERY button
   and you will get the following screen (there
   should be no errors in the Status Area):

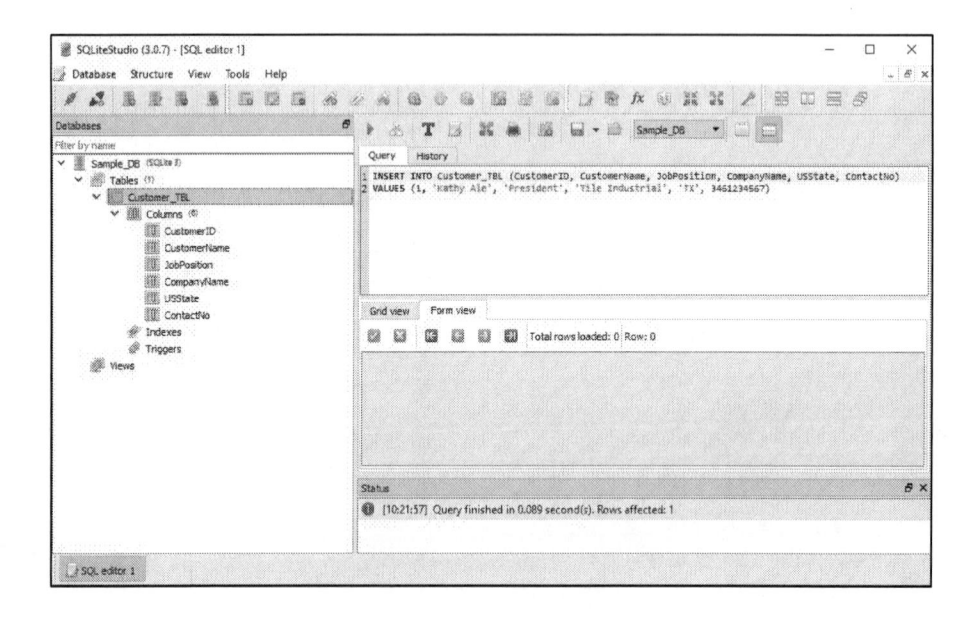

3. To check if the record of data was inserted in
   the table, double-click **Customer_TBL** at the
   left pane. Click the DATA tab at the right
   pane, which is in between STRUCTURE and
   CONSTRAINTS tabs. Your table should be
   similar to what is shown in the screen below:

CustomerID	CustomerName	JobPosition	CompanyName	USState	ContactNo
1	Kathy Ale	President	Tile Industrial	TX	3461234567

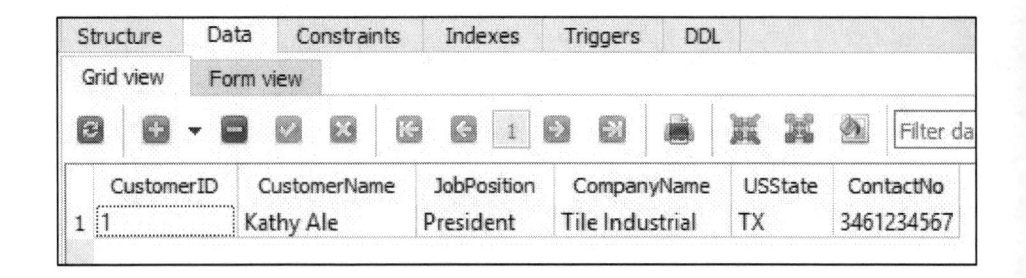

4. Click the **SQL editor 1** option at the bottom left corner of the screen. To add another record without specifying the column names, delete the programming codes inside the QUERY tab and type the following lines:

INSERT INTO Customer_TBL
VALUES (2, 'Kevin Lord', 'VP', 'Best Tooling', 'NY', 5181234567)

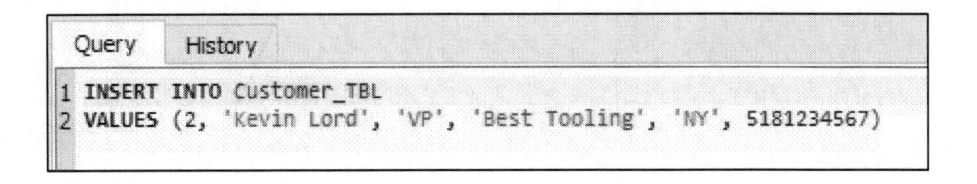

```
1 INSERT INTO Customer_TBL
2 VALUES (2, 'Kevin Lord', 'VP', 'Best Tooling', 'NY', 5181234567)
```

5. Click the EXECUTE QUERY button and provided that the order of the values corresponds exactly to the order of the **Customer_TBL** table's columns, then there should be no errors in the Status Area.

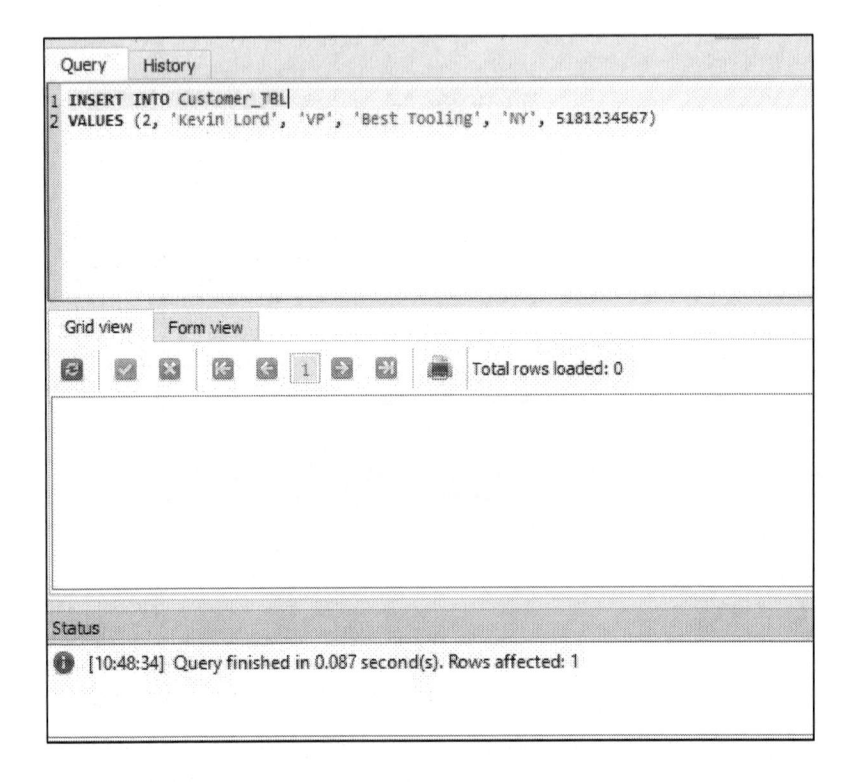

```
Query    History
1 INSERT INTO Customer_TBL
2 VALUES (2, 'Kevin Lord', 'VP', 'Best Tooling', 'NY', 5181234567)
```

Grid view   Form view

Total rows loaded: 0

Status

[10:48:34] Query finished in 0.087 second(s). Rows affected: 1

6. Click the CUSTOMER_TBL (SAMPLE_DB) option

72

Customer_TBL (Sample_DB)

at the bottom- left corner of the screen. Under the GRID VIEW tab, click the REFRESH TABLE DATA button or press F5 on your keyboard. You should see the new record added to the table.

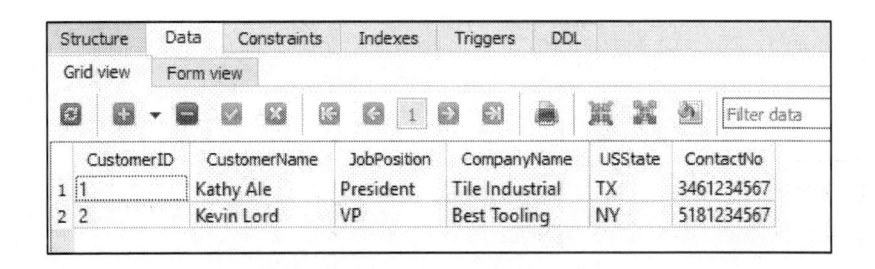

	CustomerID	CustomerName	JobPosition	CompanyName	USState	ContactNo
1	1	Kathy Ale	President	Tile Industrial	TX	3461234567
2	2	Kevin Lord	VP	Best Tooling	NY	5181234567

- **Multiple Rows at a Time**

Multiple inserts are beneficial if you need to enter a number of records into your table. This process is also more efficient rather than inserting one record at a time. All you need to do is repeat the clause following the VALUES statement, and make sure you separate them with a comma.

To insert the two remaining records into our Customer_TBL (see Chapter 2 for the details) :

1. Going back to the SQL Editor, enter the following lines of codes (without specifying the column names anymore):

    INSERT INTO Customer_TBL
    VALUES
    (3, 'Kim Ash', 'Director', 'Car World', 'CA', 5101234567),
    (4, 'Abby Karr', 'Manager', 'West Mart', 'NV', 7751234567)

2. Click the EXECUTE QUERY button .

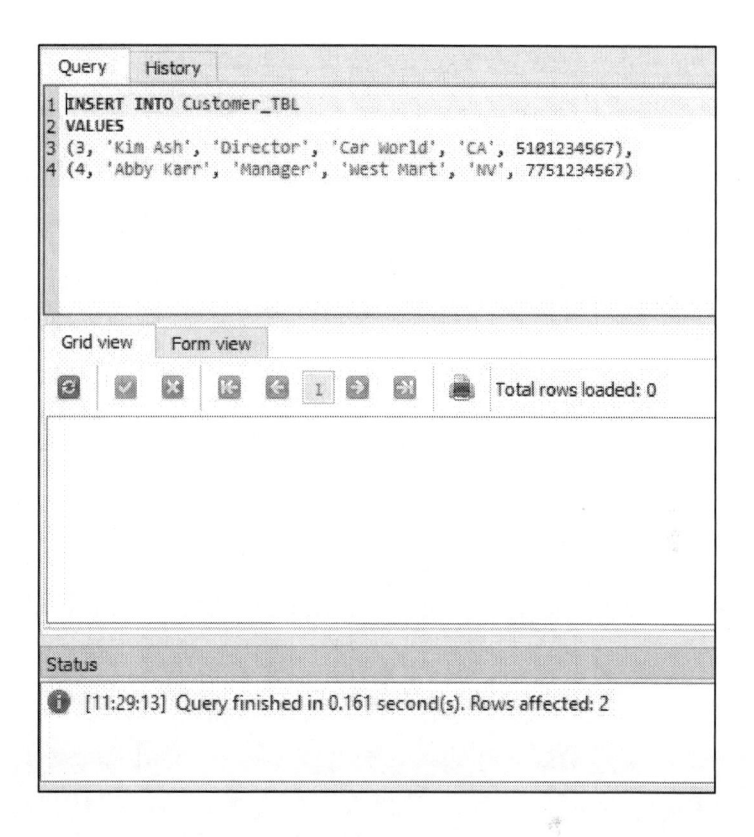

3. Go to the

Customer_TBL (Sample_DB) option.

Make sure to click the REFRESH TABLE DATA button or press F5 on your keyboard. You should now see two more records inserted to the database table.

	CustomerID	CustomerName	JobPosition	CompanyName	USState	ContactNo
1	1	Kathy Ale	President	Tile Industrial	TX	3461234567
2	2	Kevin Lord	VP	Best Tooling	NY	5181234567
3	3	Kim Ash	Director	Car World	CA	5101234567
4	4	Abby Karr	Manager	West Mart	NV	7751234567

- **Only Selected Columns at a Time**

In Chapter 5, the JobPosition field of **Customer_TBL** table was defined to allow null values. If in case you have a new customer but you do not know his position yet in the company, then you can leave the JobPosition field blank while providing the necessary information for the rest of the fields.

To add a new record without providing data for the JobPosition field:

1. Enter the following SQL lines (make sure you indicate the column names):

76

INSERT INTO Customer_TBL (CustomerID, CustomerName, CompanyName, USState, ContactNo)
VALUES (5, 'Mike Armhs', '1 Driving School', 'NJ', 2011234567)

```
1 INSERT INTO Customer_TBL (CustomerID, CustomerName, CompanyName, USState, ContactNo)
2 VALUES (5, 'Mike Armhs', '1 Driving School', 'NJ', 2011234567)
```

2. Click the EXECUTE QUERY button on top of the QUERY tab.

3. Go to the Customer_TBL (Sample_DB) option then click the REFRESH TABLE DATA button or press F5 on your keyboard. Notice that since you did not provide any information for the JobPosition field, it contains a NULL value.

	CustomerID	CustomerName	JobPosition	CompanyName	USState	ContactNo
1	1	Kathy Ale	President	Tile Industrial	TX	3461234567
2	2	Kevin Lord	VP	Best Tooling	NY	5181234567
3	3	Kim Ash	Director	Car World	CA	5101234567
4	4	Abby Karr	Manager	West Mart	NV	7751234567
5	5	Mike Armhs	NULL	1 Driving School	NJ	2011234567

UPDATE Statement

Since change is inevitable, SQL provides a way for you to update existing data stored in your database. Depending on your needs, you can modify a single record or multiple records at one time using the UPDATE command. However, only one table is generally updated at a time in a given database. The standard syntax for this DML statement is:

UPDATE *TABLE_NAME*
    SET column_1 = *EXPRESSION_1*,
        column_2 = *EXPRESSION_2*,
        ...
        column_n = *EXPRESSION_N*
    [WHERE predicates];

Again, anything inside the brackets that is indicated in the WHERE clause statement is optional and the maximum number of columns is represented by "n". The said clause identifies which rows need to be updated - this means that if the WHERE clause is not present then all the records of the table are automatically modified.

- **One Record at a Time**

　　　　From the previous discussion, you added a record of customer information without providing data for the JobPosition field. If in case you have learned that the contact person is the vice-president of the company, then you can modify this existing record.

1. Go back to the SQL EDITOR by clicking the [SQL editor 1] option. Enter the following lines of code:

   UPDATE Customer_TBL
   　SET JobPosition = 'VP'
   　WHERE CustomerName = 'Mike Armhs';

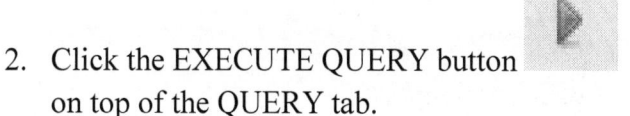

2. Click the EXECUTE QUERY button on top of the QUERY tab.

79

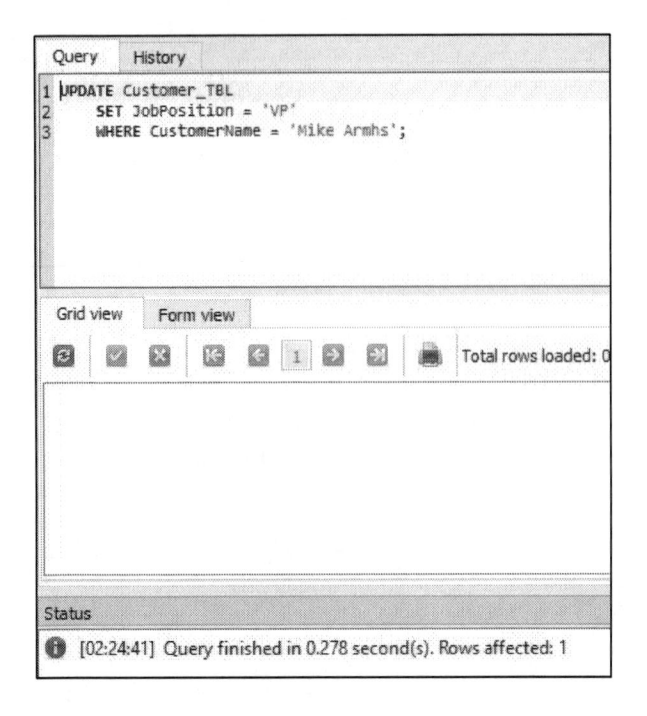

3. Click the **Customer_TBL (Sample_DB)** option then click the REFRESH TABLE DATA button or press F5 on your keyboard. You will now see 'VP' under the JobPosition field for the customer named Mike Armhs.

	CustomerID	CustomerName	JobPosition	CompanyName	USState	ContactNo
1	1	Kathy Ale	President	Tile Industrial	TX	3461234567
2	2	Kevin Lord	VP	Best Tooling	NY	5181234567
3	3	Kim Ash	Director	Car World	CA	5101234567
4	4	Abby Karr	Manager	West Mart	NV	7751234567
5	5	Mike Armhs	VP	1 Driving School	NJ	2011234567

- **Multiple Records at a Time**

Now, if you want to modify the 'VP' value of the JobPosition field to 'Vice-President' so it will be more comprehensible to database users, then you have to update multiple records at one time.

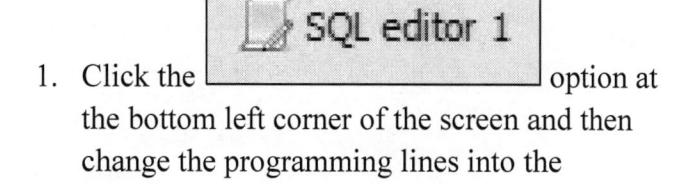

1. Click the **SQL editor 1** option at the bottom left corner of the screen and then change the programming lines into the following:

   UPDATE Customer_TBL
      SET JobPosition = 'Vice-President'

81

WHERE JobPosition = 'VP';

2. Click the EXECUTE QUERY button on top of the QUERY tab.

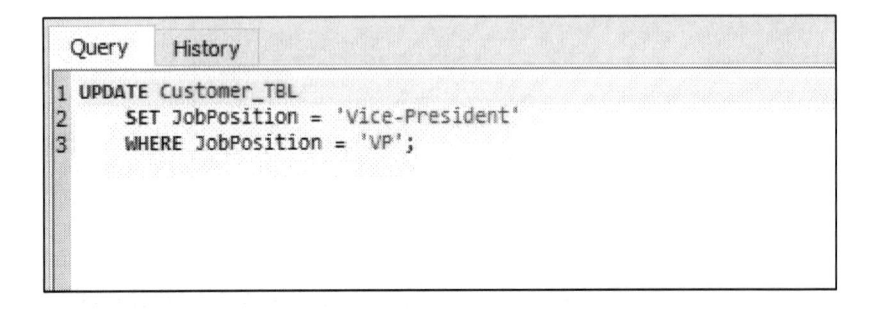

```
Query    History
1 UPDATE Customer_TBL
2     SET JobPosition = 'Vice-President'
3     WHERE JobPosition = 'VP';
```

3. Click the Customer_TBL (Sample_DB) option then click the REFRESH TABLE DATA button or press F5 on your keyboard. You should now see that the previous 'VP' value has been changed to 'Vice-President'.

82

	CustomerID	CustomerName	JobPosition	CompanyName	USState	ContactNo
1	1	Kathy Ale	President	Tile Industrial	TX	3461234567
2	2	Kevin Lord	Vice-President	Best Tooling	NY	5181234567
3	3	Kim Ash	Director	Car World	CA	5101234567
4	4	Abby Karr	Manager	West Mart	NV	7751234567
5	5	Mike Armhs	Vice-President	1 Driving School	NJ	2011234567

- **All Records at a Time**

If you want to give more emphasis to the customer name by changing it to upper case letters, then you can modify all the records of the database table at one time. In this case, you will not be needing the WHERE clause anymore.

1. Click the **SQL editor 1** option at the bottom left corner of the screen and then enter the following programming lines:

   UPDATE Customer_TBL
      SET CustomerName =
   UPPER(CustomerName)

2. Click the EXECUTE QUERY button on top of the QUERY tab.

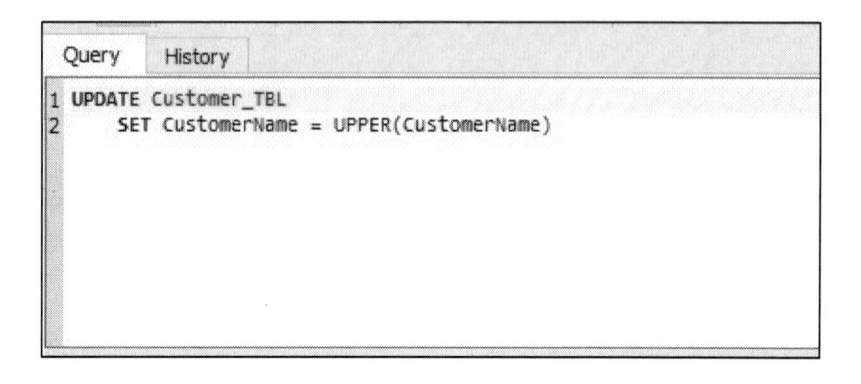

```
Query   History
1 UPDATE Customer_TBL
2     SET CustomerName = UPPER(CustomerName)
```

3. Click the Customer_TBL (Sample_DB) option then click the REFRESH TABLE DATA button or press F5 on your keyboard. Notice that the format of the customer name for all the records in the table have been changed to capital letters.

	CustomerID	CustomerName	JobPosition	CompanyName	USState	ContactNo
1	1	KATHY ALE	President	Tile Industrial	TX	3461234567
2	2	KEVIN LORD	Vice-President	Best Tooling	NY	5181234567
3	3	KIM ASH	Director	Car World	CA	5101234567
4	4	ABBY KARR	Manager	West Mart	NV	7751234567
5	5	MIKE ARMHS	Vice-President	1 Driving School	NJ	2011234567

DELETE Statement

The DELETE statement is a DML command that will remove records from a table but will still keep its existence in the database. This happens when you don't need a particular information in your database, either because they are obsolete or have no use anymore. Thus, you can free up some storage space. You can execute the DELETE command to remove just one record, multiple records or even all the records of the table at one time. Just a reminder, this command does not delete values from a specific column, but removes an entire row or a full record. That is why you have to be very careful when executing this command. There is a possibility that the effect of the DELETE command is permanent and you may not be able to recover the erased data. The standard syntax for this DML statement is:

DELETE FROM *TABLE_NAME*
[WHERE *CONDITION*];

Even if the WHERE clause is an optional part, you are required to include it when you want to delete selected rows of data from a certain table. Without the WHERE clause, you will be removing all the records from the table.

To demonstrate the function of the DELETE statement, you will create a copy of the Customer_TBL table first. In this way, you will still be able keep the original table to be used for further exercises.

1. Go to the DATABASE NAVIGATOR then right-click on **Customer_TBL**. Choose CREATE A SIMILAR TABLE.

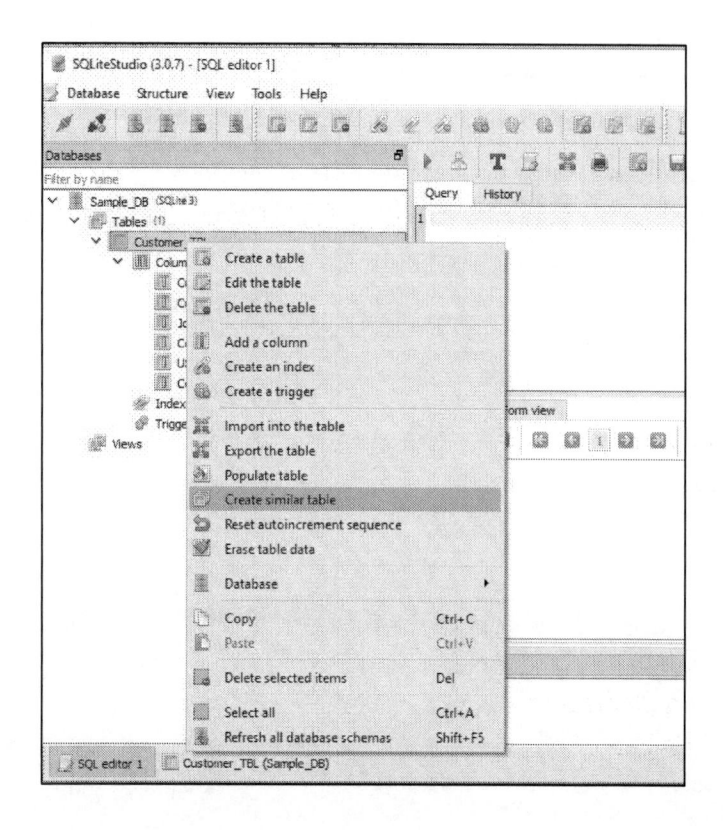

2. You will be asked to provide a name for your table. Type **Customer_TBL2** inside the TABLE NAME input box.

	Name	Data type	P	F	U	H	N	C	Default value
1	CustomerID	INTEGER	🔑				●		NULL
2	CustomerName	VARCHAR					●		NULL
3	JobPosition	VARCHAR							NULL
4	CompanyName	VARCHAR					●		NULL
5	USState	VARCHAR					●		NULL
6	ContactNo	BIGINTEGER					●		NULL

Table name: Customer_TBL2   ☐ WITHOUT ROWID

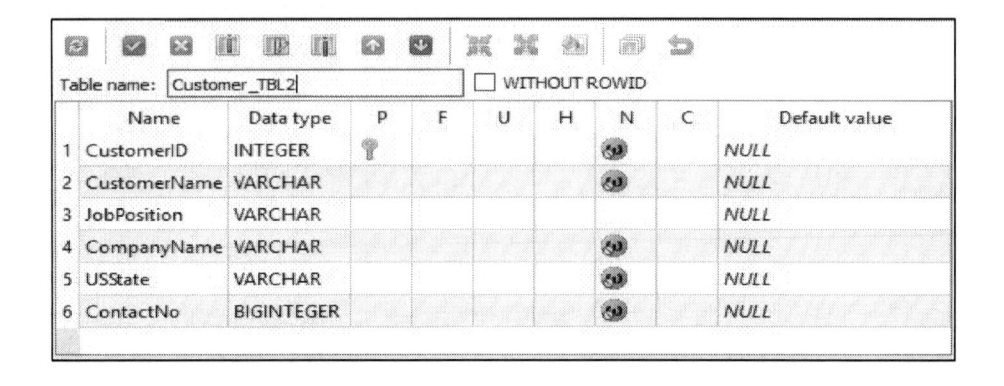

3. Click on the COMMIT STRUCTURE CHANGES button under the STRUCTURE tab. You will get the screen below.

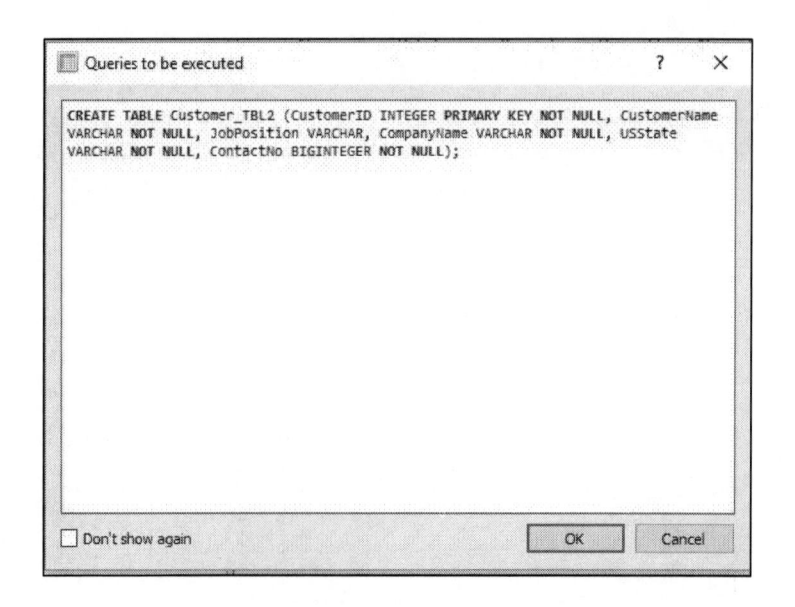

Queries to be executed

```
CREATE TABLE Customer_TBL2 (CustomerID INTEGER PRIMARY KEY NOT NULL, CustomerName
VARCHAR NOT NULL, JobPosition VARCHAR, CompanyName VARCHAR NOT NULL, USState
VARCHAR NOT NULL, ContactNo BIGINTEGER NOT NULL);
```

☐ Don't show again   [OK]   [Cancel]

4. Click on the OK button and a new **Customer_TBL2** table will be created. This will be the table that you will work around to demonstrate the DELETE command.

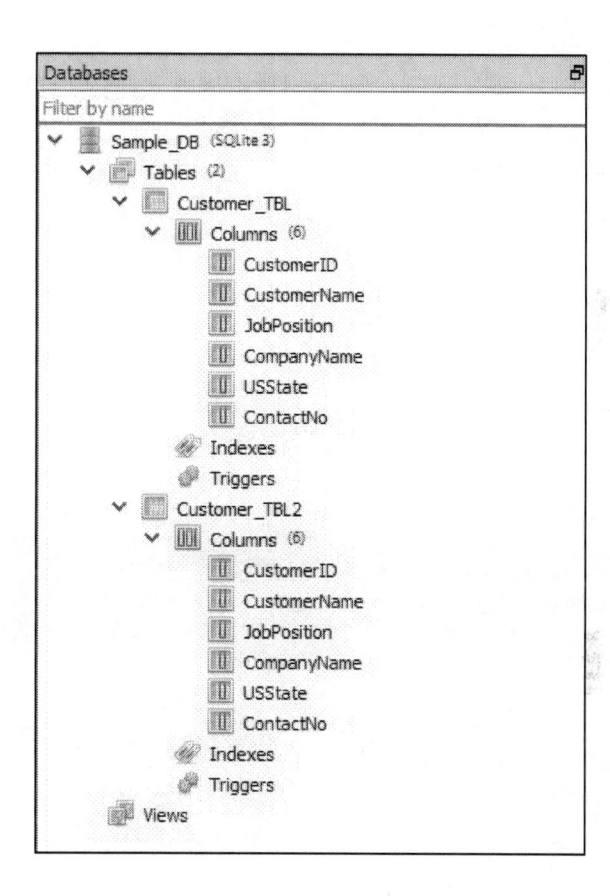

```
Databases
Filter by name
  Sample_DB (SQLite 3)
    Tables (2)
      Customer_TBL
        Columns (6)
          CustomerID
          CustomerName
          JobPosition
          CompanyName
          USState
          ContactNo
        Indexes
        Triggers
      Customer_TBL2
        Columns (6)
          CustomerID
          CustomerName
          JobPosition
          CompanyName
          USState
          ContactNo
        Indexes
        Triggers
    Views
```

At this point in time Customer_TBL2 table is empty, so you have to copy the records from Customer_TBL table. To do this, follow the steps below:

1. Click the **Customer_TBL (Sample_DB)** option then click the REFRESH TABLE DATA button  or press F5 on your keyboard. This will ensure that your data in the database table is updated.

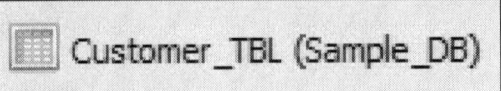

2. Click on top of the first row, just before the **CustomerID** column heading. This will highlight all the records in the table.

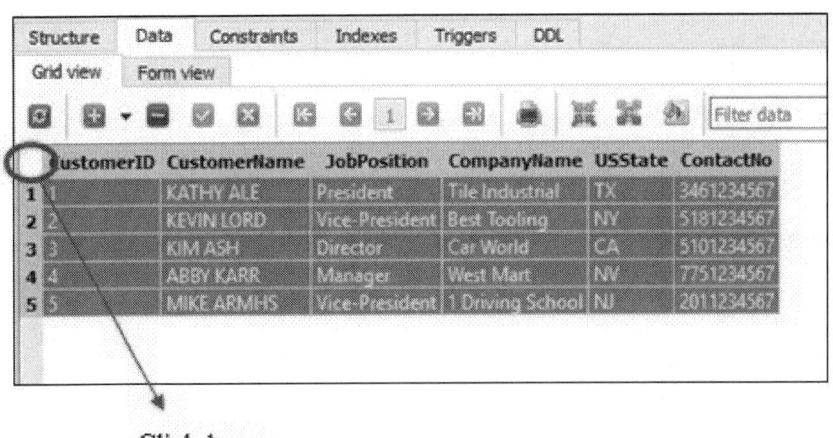

Click here

3. To copy the values, right-click on the first highlighted cell (just under the **CustomerID** column) then choose COPY.

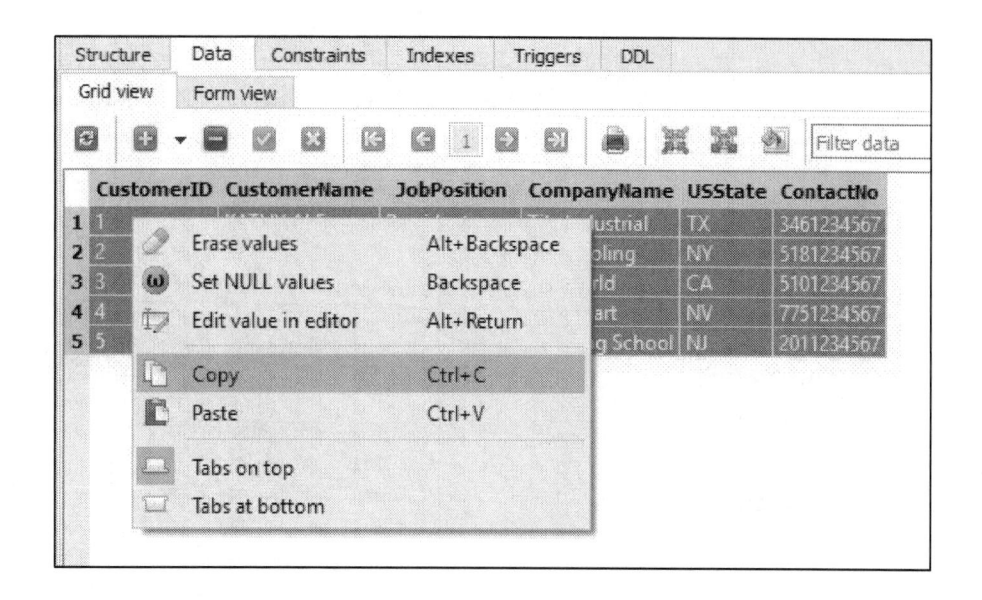

4. Double-click on **Customer_TBL2** located in the left pane. Click the DATA tab and make sure that you are on the GRID VIEW tab. You will see the same columns as in the original table, which you will be populating with the data you copied from the **Customer_TBL** table.

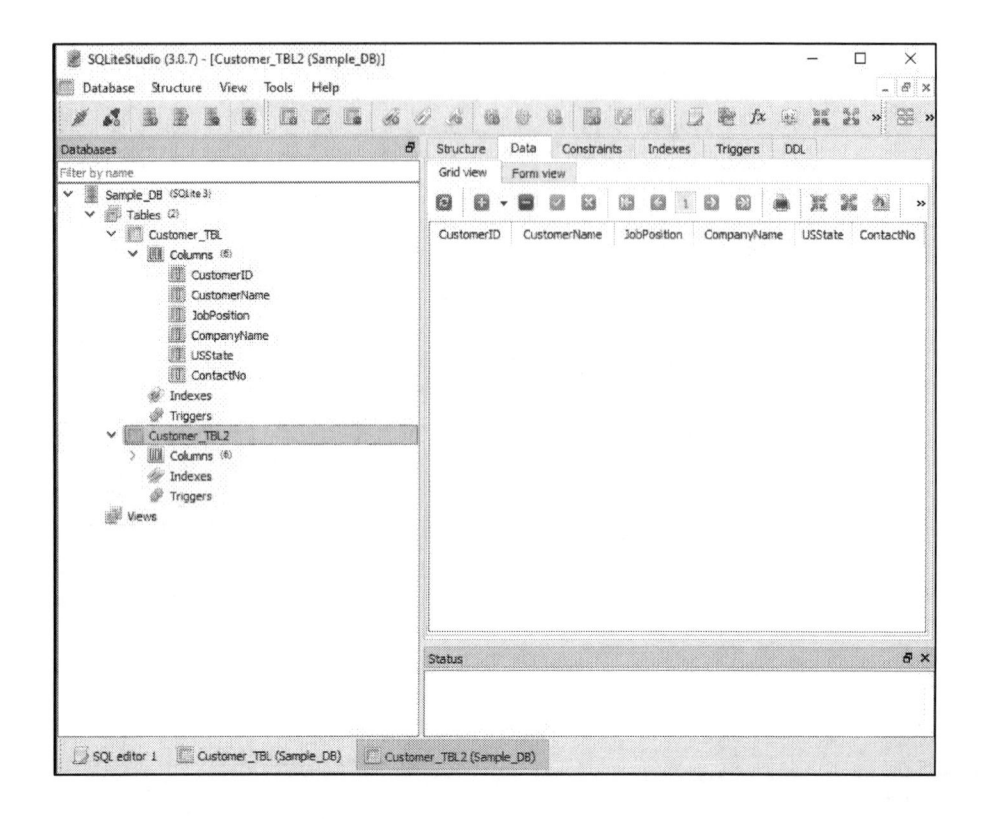

5. Click the drop- down arrow beside the INSERT ROW button (just below the GRID VIEW tab). Select INSERT MULTIPLE ROWS option.

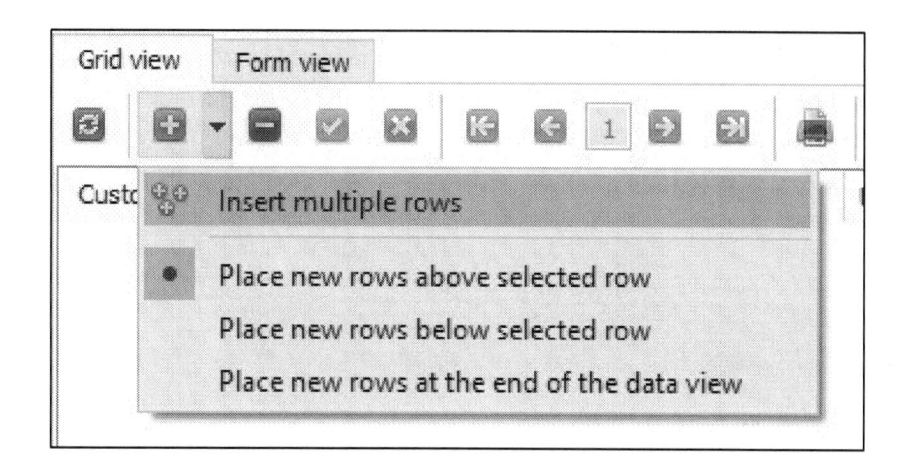

6. Inside the NUMBER OF ROWS TO INSERT input box type **5**. Click OK.

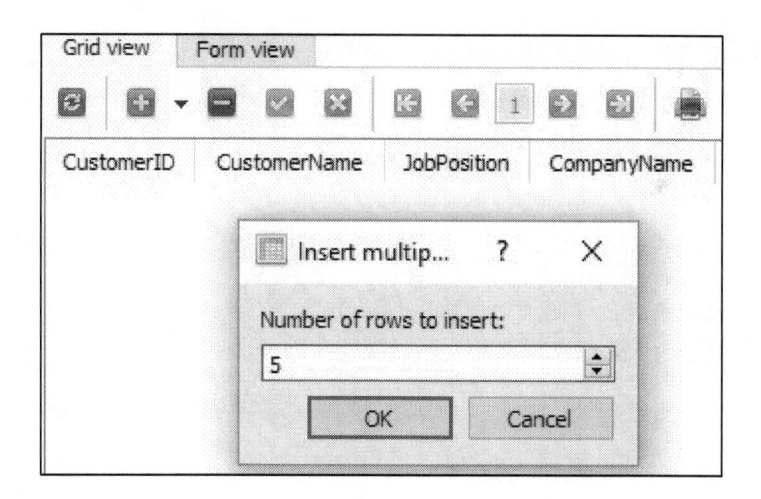

7. Your table will now have 5 rows of data that contain NULL values. This is where you will insert the values that you copied from the **Customer_TBL** table.

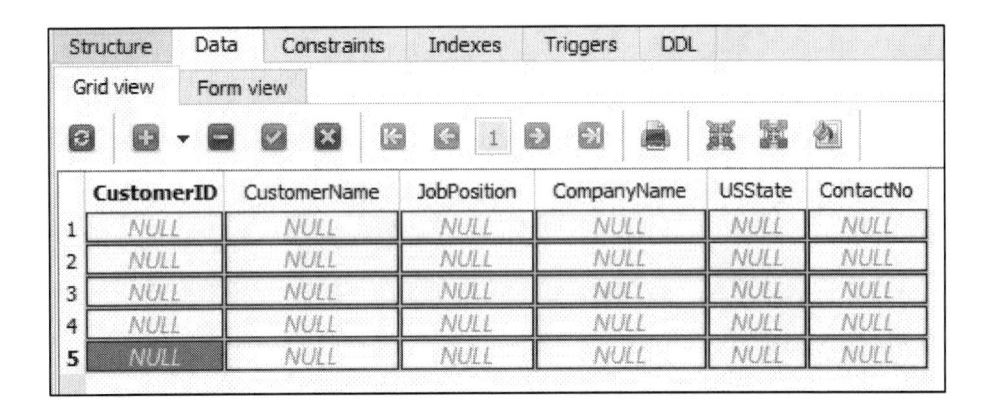

	CustomerID	CustomerName	JobPosition	CompanyName	USState	ContactNo
1	NULL	NULL	NULL	NULL	NULL	NULL
2	NULL	NULL	NULL	NULL	NULL	NULL
3	NULL	NULL	NULL	NULL	NULL	NULL
4	NULL	NULL	NULL	NULL	NULL	NULL
5	NULL	NULL	NULL	NULL	NULL	NULL

8. Right-click on the first cell then choose the PASTE option.

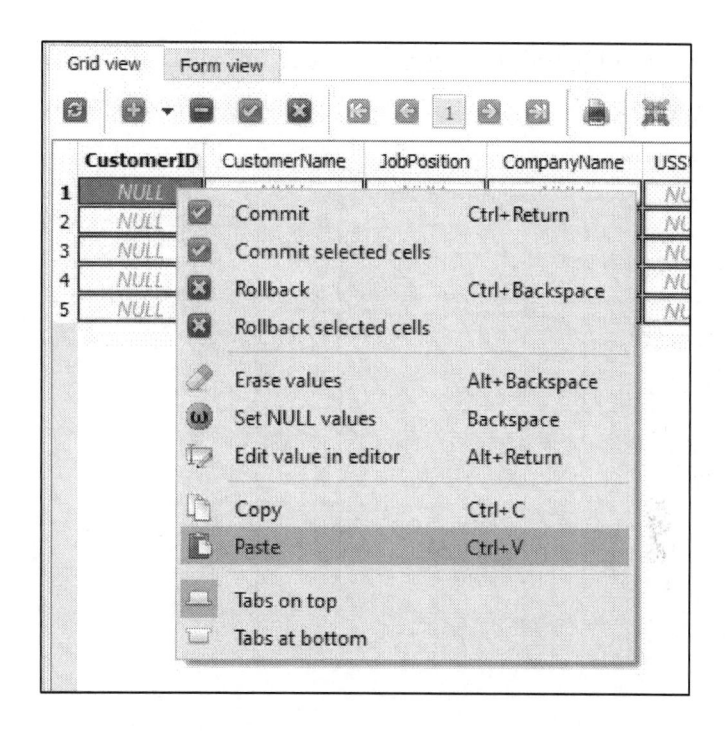

9. All the data values from the **Customer_TBL** table will be inserted to the **Customer_TBL2** table, which you will manipulate to demonstrate the DELETE command.

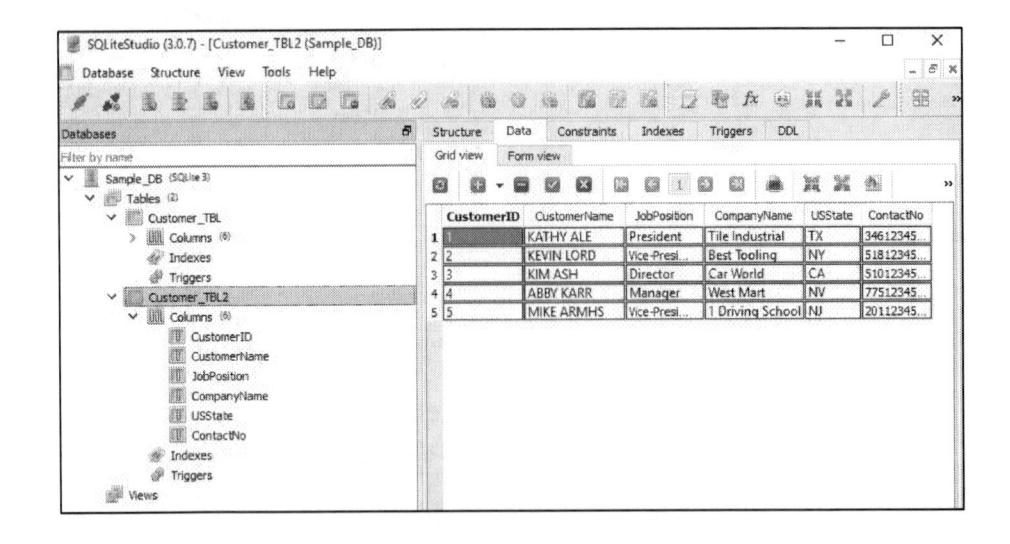

10. Click on the COMMIT STRUCTURE CHANGES button to save the data in the table.

- **Single Record**

    To delete only one record of data from the Customer_TBL2 table where the customer's name matches to 'KATHY ALE':

96

1. Click the **SQL editor 1** option, type the following lines of code in the QUERY tab and then click the EXECUTE QUERY button ▷.

   DELETE FROM Customer_TBL2
   WHERE CustomerName = 'KATHY ALE';

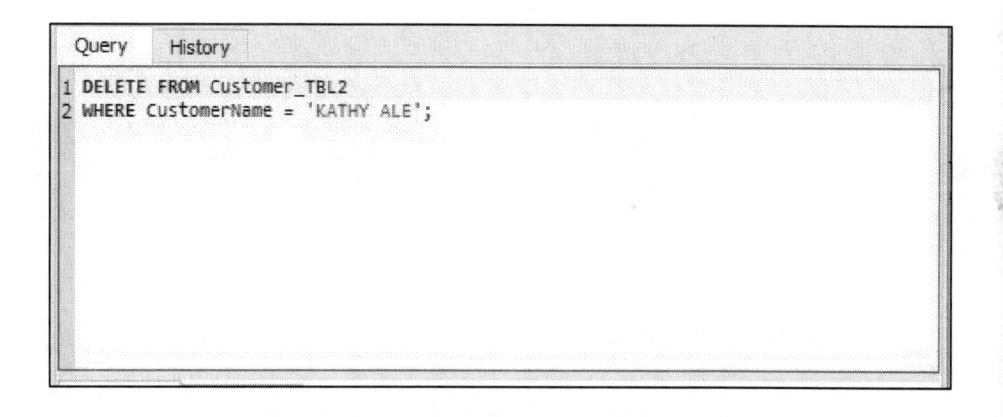

   ```
   1 DELETE FROM Customer_TBL2
   2 WHERE CustomerName = 'KATHY ALE';
   ```

2. To check if the record has been deleted, go to the **Customer_TBL2** table by clicking on **Customer_TBL2 (Sample_DB)**.

   Then click on the REFRESH TABLE DATA

button ![refresh] or press F5 on your keyboard to update the values. You will notice that the record has been deleted already.

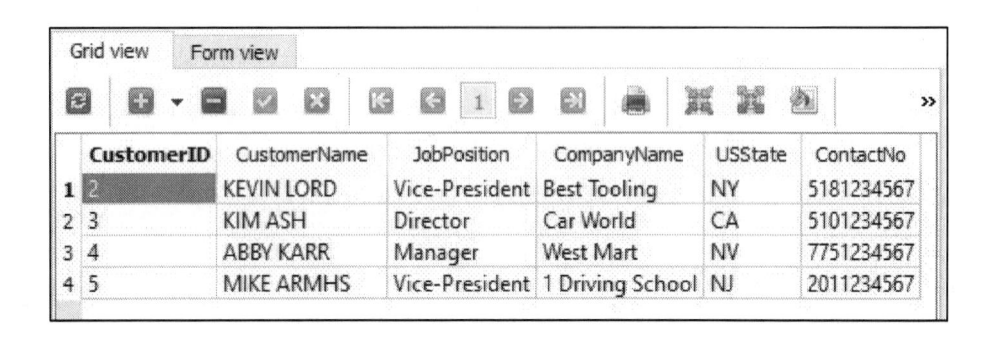

	CustomerID	CustomerName	JobPosition	CompanyName	USState	ContactNo
1	2	KEVIN LORD	Vice-President	Best Tooling	NY	5181234567
2	3	KIM ASH	Director	Car World	CA	5101234567
3	4	ABBY KARR	Manager	West Mart	NV	7751234567
4	5	MIKE ARMHS	Vice-President	1 Driving School	NJ	2011234567

- **Multiple Records**

To delete 2 records of data from the Customer_TBL2 table where the customer's position matches to 'Vice-President':

1. Click the ![SQL editor 1] option, type the following lines of code and then click the EXECUTE QUERY button ![▶] .

DELETE FROM Customer_TBL2
WHERE JobPosition = 'Vice-President';

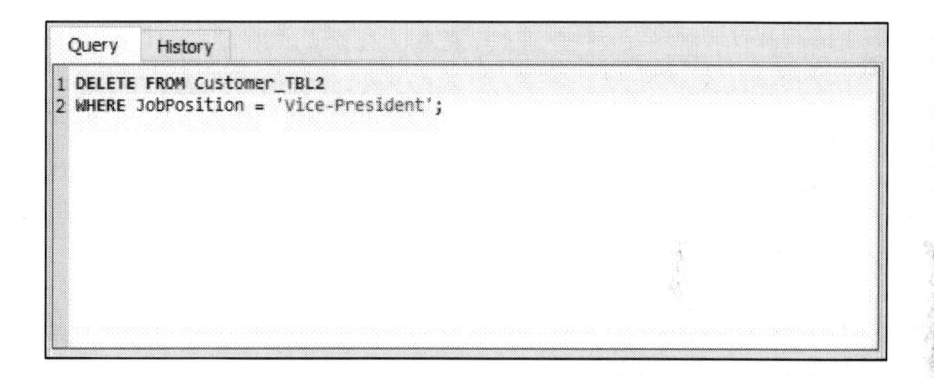

```
1 DELETE FROM Customer_TBL2
2 WHERE JobPosition = 'Vice-President';
```

2. To check if the record has been deleted, go to the **Customer_TBL2** table by clicking on

    Customer_TBL2 (Sample_DB)

    Then click on the REFRESH TABLE DATA button or press **F5** on your keyboard to update the values. You will notice that the two records have been deleted already.

99

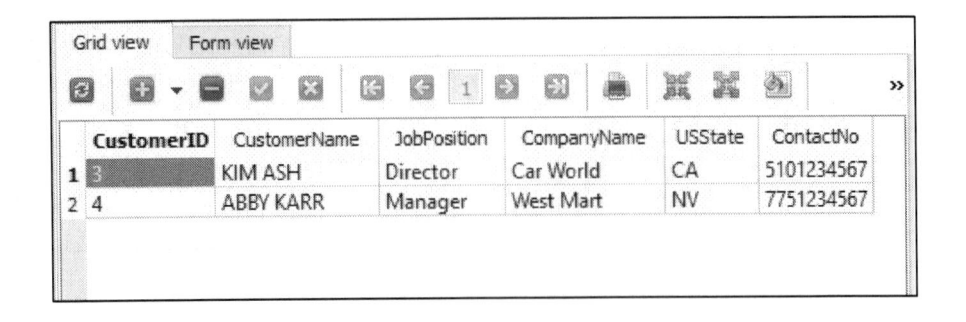

	CustomerID	CustomerName	JobPosition	CompanyName	USState	ContactNo
1	3	KIM ASH	Director	Car World	CA	5101234567
2	4	ABBY KARR	Manager	West Mart	NV	7751234567

- **Whole Table**

    To delete all the remaining records from the Customer_TBL2 table at one time:

    1. Click the **SQL editor 1** option, type the following lines of code in the QUERY tab and then click the EXECUTE QUERY button.

    DELETE FROM Customer_TBL2

```
Query   History
1 DELETE FROM Customer_TBL2
```

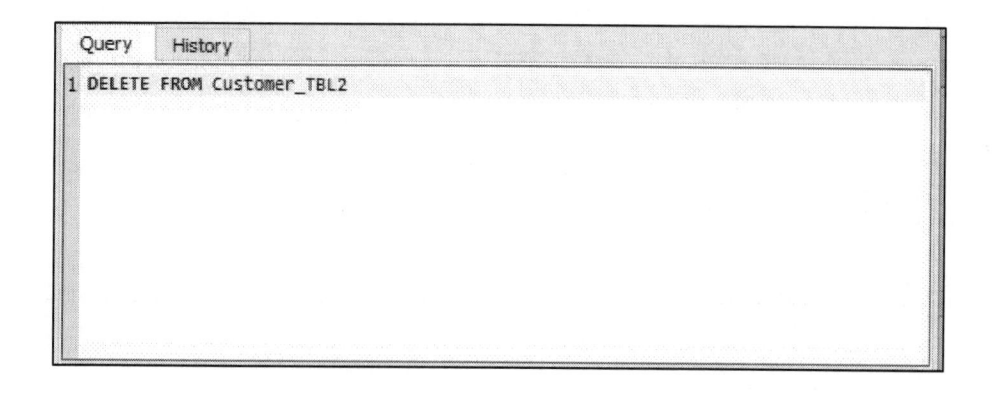

2. To check if the record has been deleted, go to the Customer_TBL2 table by clicking on `Customer_TBL2 (Sample_DB)`. Then click on the REFRESH TABLE DATA button or press F5 on your keyboard to update the values. You will notice that executing the single DELETE command has deleted all the records from the table.

In this chapter, you have learned how to encode programming lines using the most commonly used DML command statements in inserting, updating and deleting records from database tables in SQL. In the next chapter, you will learn the different DQL commands that will allow you to retrieve valuable information contained in database tables.

Chapter Seven: Data Query Language Statements

In this chapter, you will learn how to use the available Data Query Language statements in retrieving data from database tables. Through SQLiteStudio, you will be able to use SELECT, WHERE, ORDER BY and GROUP BY statements in requesting and displaying significant database information.

Once you have created and populated your tables with data values, there will come a time that you will need to perform database queries to retrieve relevant information. A query is a valid inquiry into the database to extract and display data in a readable or understandable format, depending on the user's request. The main challenge in SQL is to correctly instruct the computer what to search for by manipulating the database through row selection. Once you have selected the values you need then you can further perform various operations such as data addition, deletion, modification and more.

SELECT Statement

Retrieving data values is the most performed manipulation task by database users. In doing such operation, you need to use the DML command statement called SELECT. You have the option to retrieve just one row, a number of rows or all the rows of the database table.

Using the SELECT statement in retrieving all the records of a particular table is the basic form of this DML command statement. Even if the SELECT command is considered to be the most powerful statement, it requires other clauses to function correctly in performing a query. The syntax in its simplest form is:

SELECT * FROM *TABLE_NAME*;

In the programming line above, the asterisk sign (*) signifies everything. This means that the wildcard character is a shortcut for the listing of all the column names of a particular table.

To select all the data rows from the Customer_TBL table:

1. Click the **SQL editor 1** option and then type the following lines of code:

SELECT * FROM Customer_TBL;

2. Click the EXECUTE QUERY button . The result of this SELECT command is displayed inside the GRID VIEW tab.

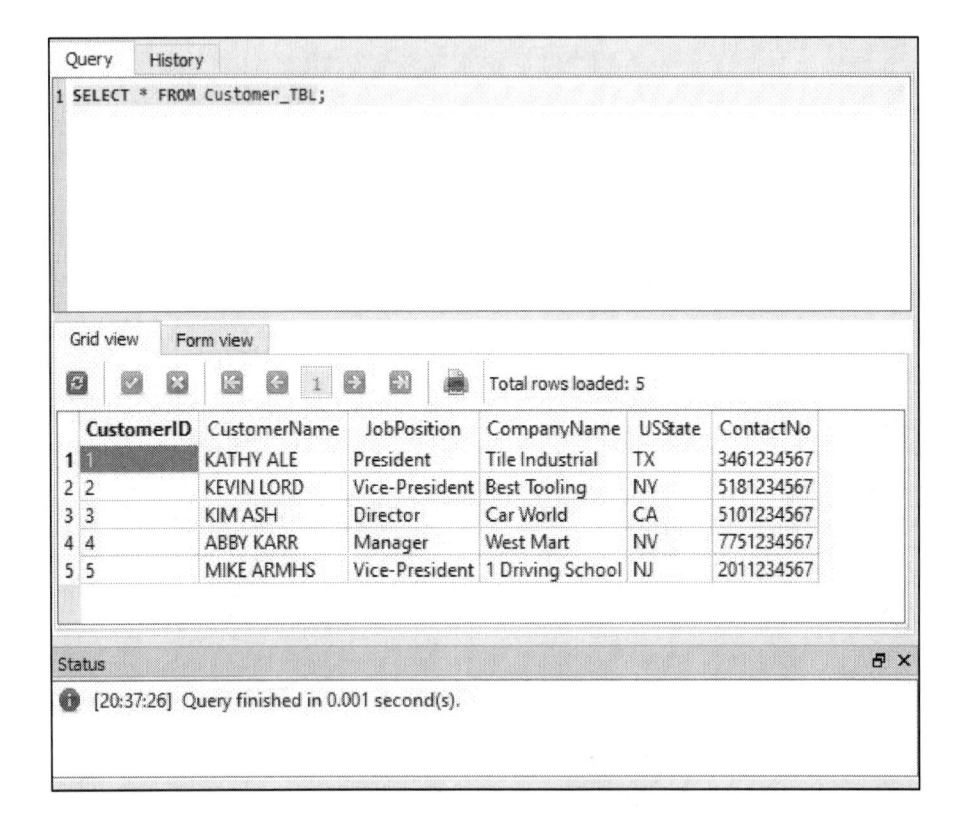

CustomerID	CustomerName	JobPosition	CompanyName	USState	ContactNo
1	KATHY ALE	President	Tile Industrial	TX	3461234567
2	KEVIN LORD	Vice-President	Best Tooling	NY	5181234567
3	KIM ASH	Director	Car World	CA	5101234567
4	ABBY KARR	Manager	West Mart	NV	7751234567
5	MIKE ARMHS	Vice-President	1 Driving School	NJ	2011234567

The result basically shows the entire data of the Customer_TBL table since the code instructs the database to select all the rows and columns of the said table.

WHERE Statement

When you want to be more specific in selecting rows of data from your database tables, then you need to add a bit of complexity to your programming lines. At this point, you need the function of the WHERE clause, which means that the SELECT operation will be performed once the stated condition inside such clause is true. The syntax of the SELECT statement with the WHERE clause is as follows:

SELECT *COLUMN_LIST*
FROM *TABLE_NAME*
WHERE *CONDITION;*

To select only the rows of data where the job position of the customer is Vice-President:

1. Click the **SQL editor 1** option and then type the following lines of code:

SELECT *
FROM Customer_TBL
WHERE JobPosition = 'Vice-President';

2. Click the EXECUTE QUERY button ![play]. The result of this SELECT command is displayed inside the GRID VIEW tab.

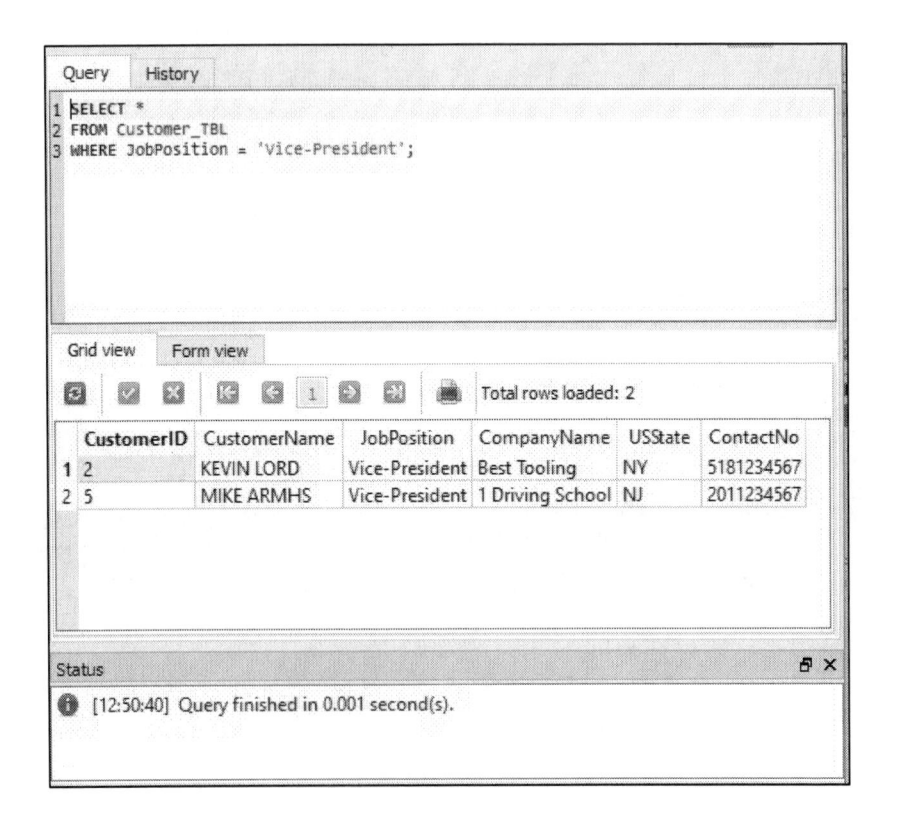

```
Query   History
1 SELECT *
2 FROM Customer_TBL
3 WHERE JobPosition = 'Vice-President';
```

Grid view | Form view

Total rows loaded: 2

	CustomerID	CustomerName	JobPosition	CompanyName	USState	ContactNo
1	2	KEVIN LORD	Vice-President	Best Tooling	NY	5181234567
2	5	MIKE ARMHS	Vice-President	1 Driving School	NJ	2011234567

Status

[12:50:40] Query finished in 0.001 second(s).

The result shows the records of the two customers named Kevin Lord and Mike Armhs who are both Vice-Presidents of their respective companies.

What if you only want to select certain columns of the table, maybe just the full name and company of the customer? You will now modify your lines of code into the following:

1. In the QUERY tab, change the wildcard character * (asterisk sign) into CustomerName and CompanyName by typing the following:

   SELECT CustomerName, CompanyName
   FROM Customer_TBL
   WHERE JobPosition = 'Vice-President';

2. Click the EXECUTE QUERY button . The result of this SELECT command is displayed inside the GRID VIEW tab.

```
Query   History
1 SELECT CustomerName, CompanyName
2 FROM Customer_TBL
3 WHERE JobPosition = 'Vice-President';
```

Grid view | Form view

Total rows loaded: 2

	CustomerName	CompanyName
1	KEVIN LORD	Best Tooling
2	MIKE ARMHS	1 Driving School

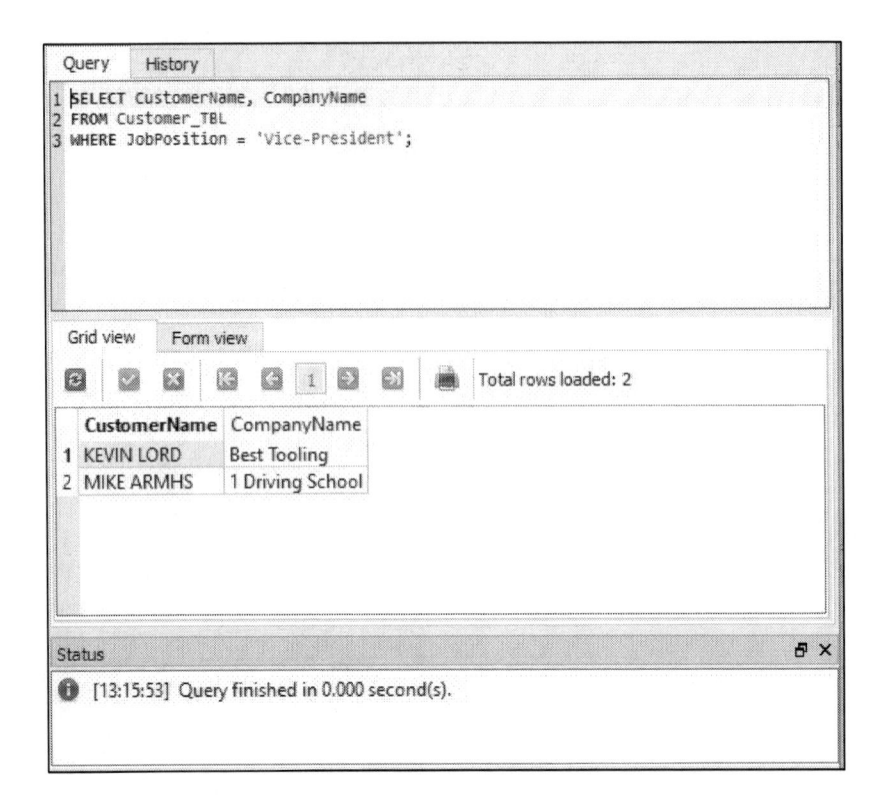

Status

[13:15:53] Query finished in 0.000 second(s).

By specifying the columns that you want to select, you are trying to customize what data you want to retrieve and how you want them to be displayed. In the previous example, you only wanted to know the customer's name and his company where the job position is vice-president.

ORDER BY and GROUP BY Statements

When you want data that you retrieve to be displayed and sorted in some way, then you need to include the ORDER BY or GROUP BY operator at the end of your SQL statement. The primary function of the ORDER BY statement is basically to arrange data using a specific order, whether ascending or descending. On the other hand, the GROUP BY statement is used to put identical data together and arrange the query output into groups.

The standard syntax for the ORDER BY clause is:

SELECT *COLUMN_LIST*
  FROM *TABLE_NAME*
  ORDER BY *COLUMN_LIST* [ASC | DESC];

By default, ORDER BY sorts individual rows in ascending order. If you want to arrange your records in descending order then you have to indicate the DESC operator at the end of the ORDER BY clause.

To retrieve all customer records from the Customer_TBL table and display them in ascending order by US state:

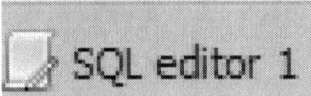

1. Click the **SQL editor 1** option and then type the following lines of code:

   SELECT *
   FROM Customer_TBL
   ORDER BY USState;

2. Click the EXECUTE QUERY button. The result of this SELECT command is displayed inside the GRID VIEW tab.

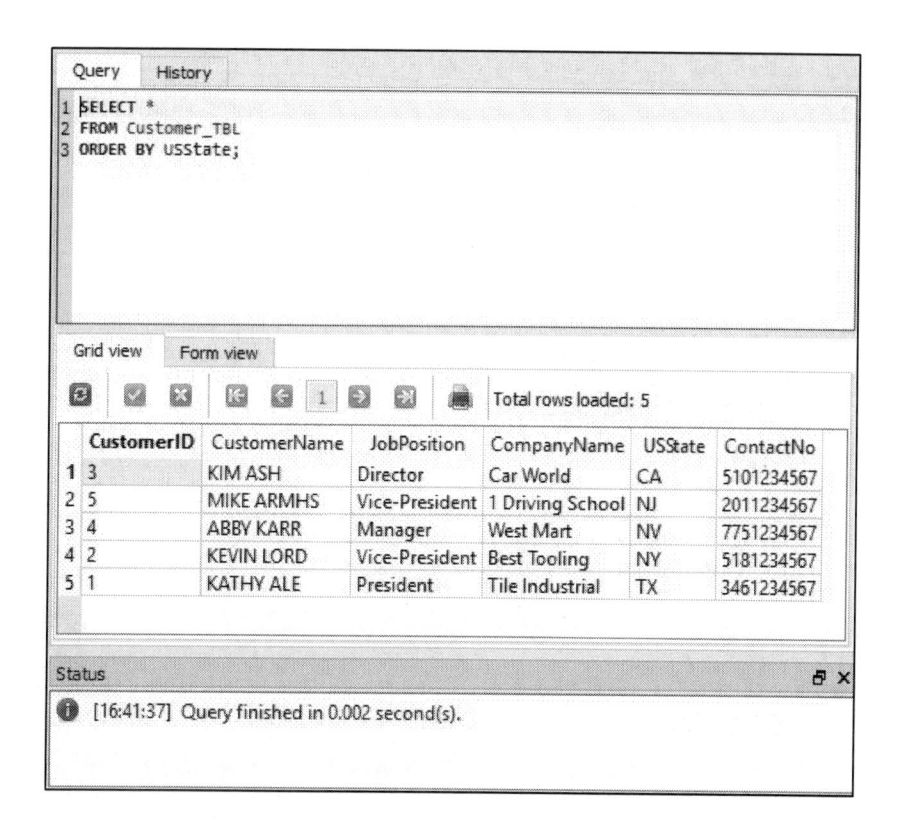

```
Query    History
1 SELECT *
2 FROM Customer_TBL
3 ORDER BY USState;
```

CustomerID	CustomerName	JobPosition	CompanyName	USState	ContactNo
3	KIM ASH	Director	Car World	CA	5101234567
5	MIKE ARMHS	Vice-President	1 Driving School	NJ	2011234567
4	ABBY KARR	Manager	West Mart	NV	7751234567
2	KEVIN LORD	Vice-President	Best Tooling	NY	5181234567
1	KATHY ALE	President	Tile Industrial	TX	3461234567

Total rows loaded: 5

[16:41:37] Query finished in 0.002 second(s).

Since you did not specify how the records will be sorted, the data rows were arranged alphabetically (in an ascending order) using the USState column. If you want to sort your records in descending order:

1. Inside the QUERY tab, add DESC after **USState** in the ORDER BY clause.

   SELECT *
   FROM Customer_TBL

ORDER BY USState DESC;

2. Click the EXECUTE QUERY button. The result of this SELECT command is displayed inside the GRID VIEW tab.

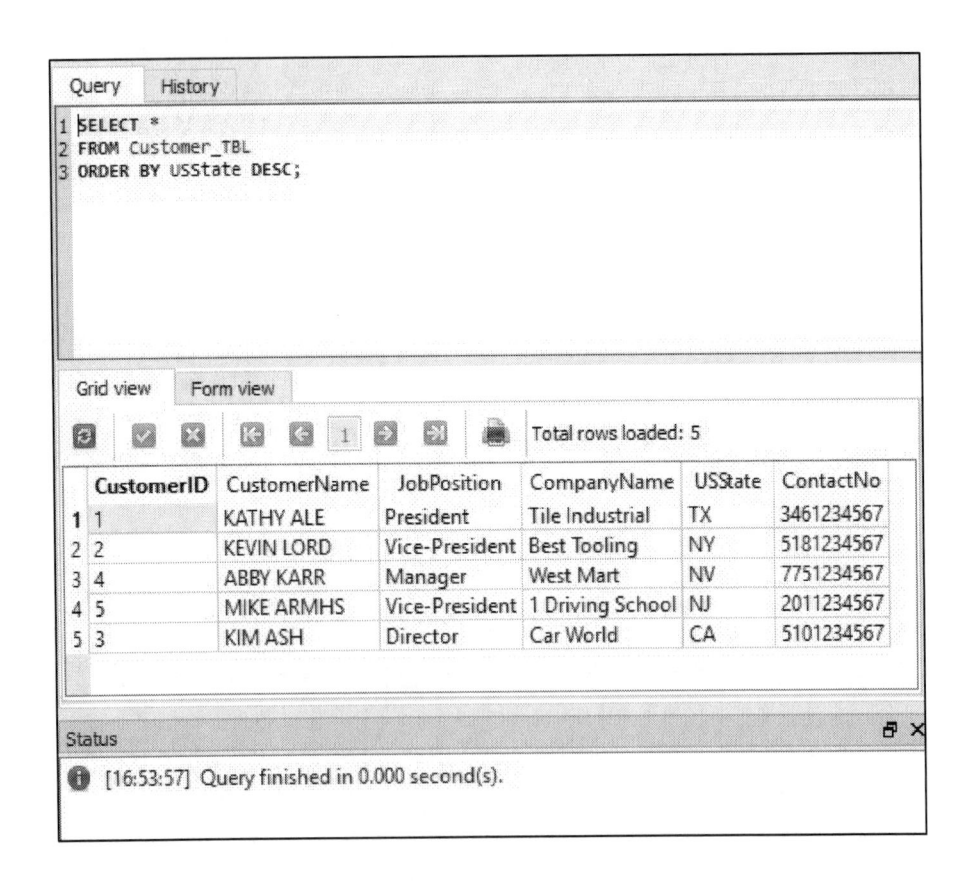

```
1 SELECT *
2 FROM Customer_TBL
3 ORDER BY USState DESC;
```

Total rows loaded: 5

CustomerID	CustomerName	JobPosition	CompanyName	USState	ContactNo
1	1	KATHY ALE	President	Tile Industrial	TX	3461234567
2	2	KEVIN LORD	Vice-President	Best Tooling	NY	5181234567
3	4	ABBY KARR	Manager	West Mart	NV	7751234567
4	5	MIKE ARMHS	Vice-President	1 Driving School	NJ	2011234567
5	3	KIM ASH	Director	Car World	CA	5101234567

Status

[16:53:57] Query finished in 0.000 second(s).

If you want to determine something about a group of records or need to combine columns with duplicate values in a logical way, then it is time to use the GROUP BY clause. Other terms similar to grouping are aggregating, summarizing and rolling up. To illustrate this, if you want to know how many customers are there for every job position in the Customer_TBL table then we need to count the number of records and display the total number of customers per job position.

1. Click the **SQL editor 1** option and then type the following lines of code:

    SELECT JobPosition, COUNT(*) AS number_of_record
    FROM Customer_TBL
    GROUP BY JobPosition;

2. Click the EXECUTE QUERY button ▶. The result of this SELECT command is displayed inside the GRID VIEW tab.

```
Query   History
1 SELECT JobPosition, COUNT(*) AS number_of_record
2 FROM Customer_TBL
3 GROUP BY JobPosition;
```

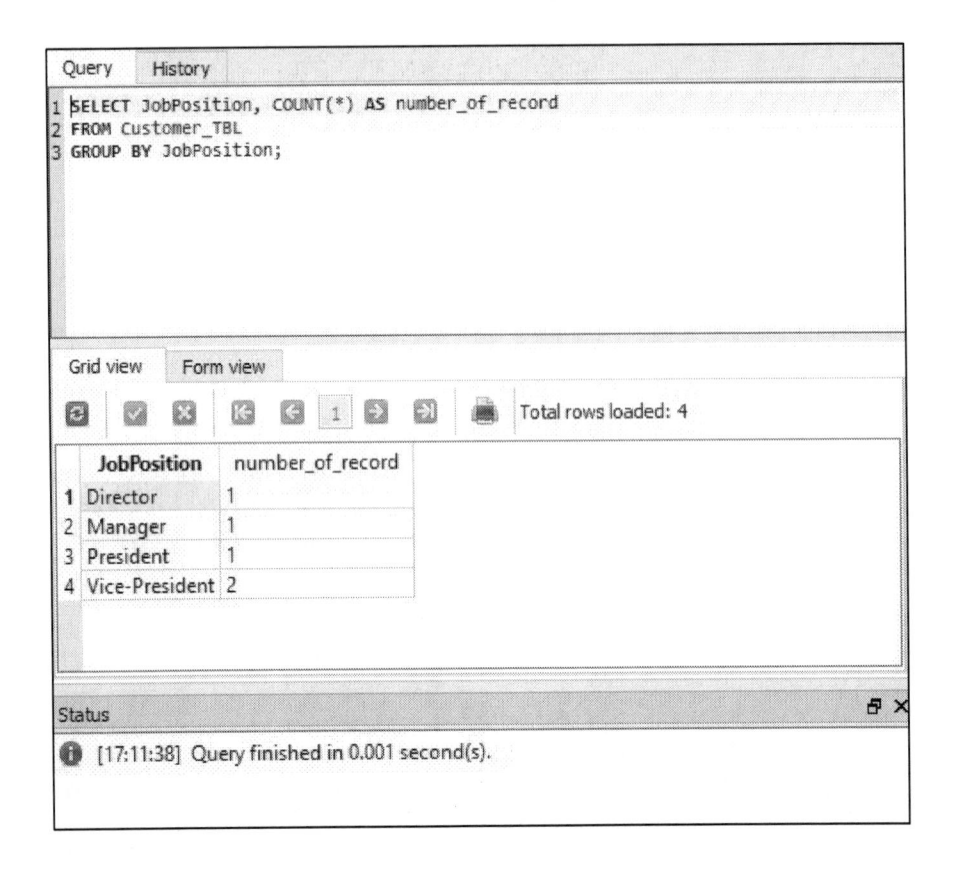

Grid view | Form view

Total rows loaded: 4

	JobPosition	number_of_record
1	Director	1
2	Manager	1
3	President	1
4	Vice-President	2

Status

[17:11:38] Query finished in 0.001 second(s).

In the example above, the COUNT function was introduced to arrange the data in groups. The following is a summary of the common aggregate functions used together with the GROUP BY statement (x denotes the column name where you want to perform the function):

- AVG(x) – computes the average of all the column values (null values removed)

- COUNT(x) – counts the number of non-null values in the column

- COUNT(*) – counts the number of records

- MAX(x) – computes the maximum value in the column (null values removed)

- MIN(x) - computes the minimum value in the column (null values removed)

- SUM(x) – computes the sum or total of the values in the column (null values ignored)

Going back to the GROUP BY example, the data in the JobPosition column is retrieved and for each instance of the value, a record is counted using the COUNT function. The number_of record is a new column created that displays the total number of records per job position. The Director, Manager and President positions have 1 record each while the Vice-President has 2. This is because there are two customers who are vice-presidents – Kevin Lord and Mike Armhs. If you can also notice, the records displayed are sorted in an ascending order by default.

Altering your SQL statements to display the job position in a descending order will require you to add the ORDER BY statement after the GROUP BY clause (ORDER BY will always come after the GROUP BY statement). Change your lines of code into the following and then click the EXECUTE QUERY button on top of the QUERY tab:

```
SELECT JobPosition, COUNT(*) AS number_of_record
    FROM Customer_TBL
    GROUP BY JobPosition
    ORDER BY JobPosition DESC;
```

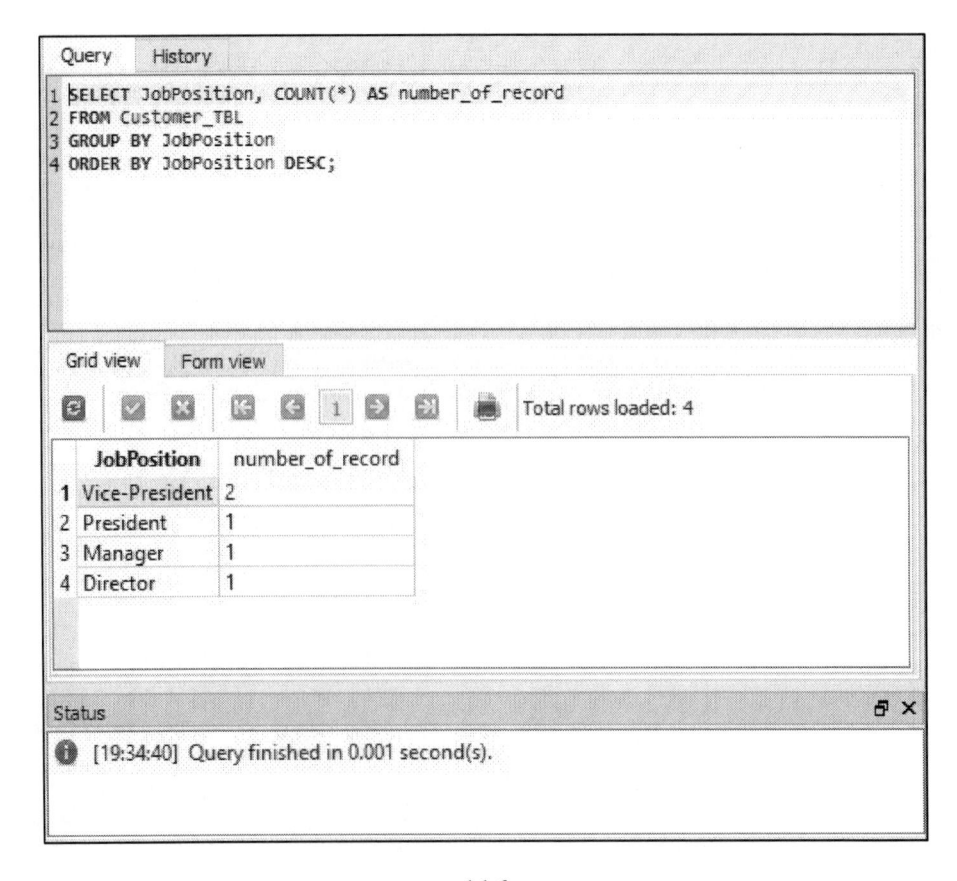

	JobPosition	number_of_record
1	Vice-President	2
2	President	1
3	Manager	1
4	Director	1

Total rows loaded: 4

Status
[19:34:40] Query finished in 0.001 second(s).

In this chapter, you have learned how to encode programming lines using the most commonly used DQL command statements in selecting, ordering and grouping records from database tables in SQL. In the next chapter, you will learn the different transactional control commands that will allow you to manage several relational database transactions.

Chapter Eight: Transactional Control Commands

In this chapter, you will learn how to use three of the available transactional control commands in a relational database management system (RDBMS) using SQLiteStudio – COMMIT, ROLLBACK and SAVEPOINT. Controlling transactions requires you to be able to manage certain database changes that are usually brought about by the insert, update and delete commands.

Executing a database transaction seems to have been successfully completed when you notice that the table's data or structure has been changed. What is actually happening during a transaction execution is that information is stored in a temporary space in the database (or what you can call a rollback area). When you want to finalize these transactions, and store the information permanently, then you either save or discard the changes made to the database tables by issuing the appropriate transactional control command. Only then that the rollback area is emptied.

COMMIT Command

Using the COMMIT command saves all the transactions into your database. Normally, in SQLiteStudio, whenever you execute a CREATE, INSERT or DELETE transaction by writing programming lines in the SQL Editor, the changes are automatically saved. You have first encountered the COMMIT command through the COMMIT CHANGES STRUCTURE button in Chapter 6, where you created a copy of the Customer_TBL table. Now, to demonstrate this command again in SQLiteStudio, you will manipulate the table structure by adding a new record to the Customer_TBL table in GRID VIEW mode.

1. Click the **SQL editor 1** option. To ensure that there are no transactions currently running in the database, type the following programming line in the QUERY tab then click the EXECUTE QUERY button:

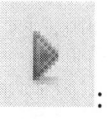

   END TRANSACTION;

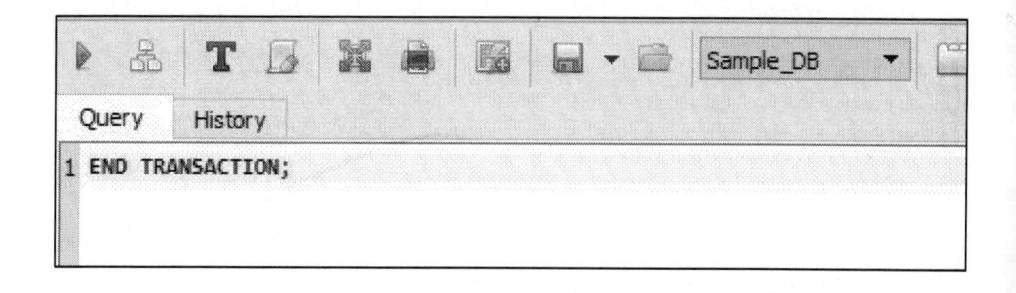

2. Double-click **Customer_TBL** under the TABLES list in the DATABASE NAVIGATOR pane. Click the DATA tab at the right and make sure that the GRID View is displayed. You will see all the records of the **Customer_TBL** table.

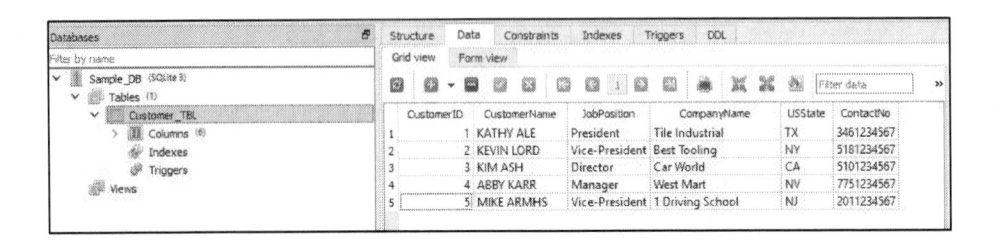

CustomerID	CustomerName	JobPosition	CompanyName	USState	ContactNo
1	KATHY ALE	President	Tile Industrial	TX	3461234567
2	KEVIN LORD	Vice-President	Best Tooling	NY	5181234567
3	KIM ASH	Director	Car World	CA	5101234567
4	ABBY KARR	Manager	West Mart	NV	7751234567
5	MIKE ARMHS	Vice-President	1 Driving School	NJ	2011234567

3. Click the first column of the last row of the table, which is **CustomerID 5**.

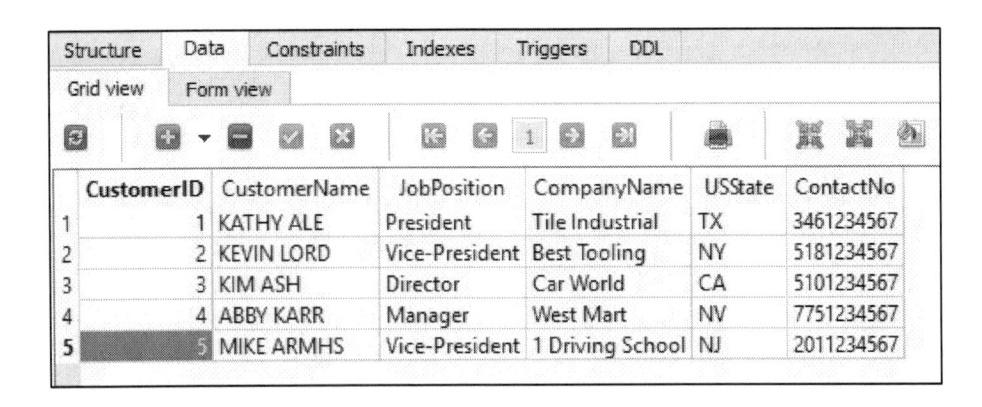

CustomerID	CustomerName	JobPosition	CompanyName	USState	ContactNo
1	KATHY ALE	President	Tile Industrial	TX	3461234567
2	KEVIN LORD	Vice-President	Best Tooling	NY	5181234567
3	KIM ASH	Director	Car World	CA	5101234567
4	ABBY KARR	Manager	West Mart	NV	7751234567
5	MIKE ARMHS	Vice-President	1 Driving School	NJ	2011234567

4. Click the drop-down arrow beside the INSERT ROW (INS) button and select PLACE NEW ROWS BELOW SELECTED ROW option.

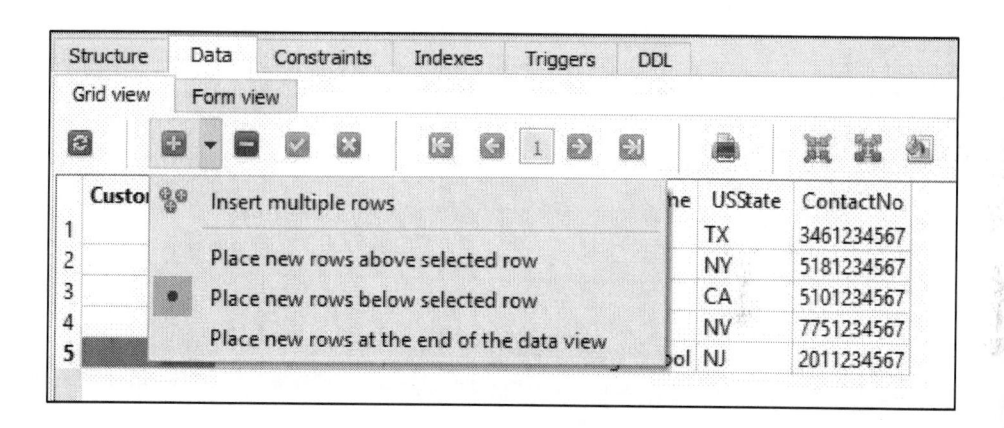

5. This time click the INSERT ROW (INS) button and you will see a new empty row added to the table.

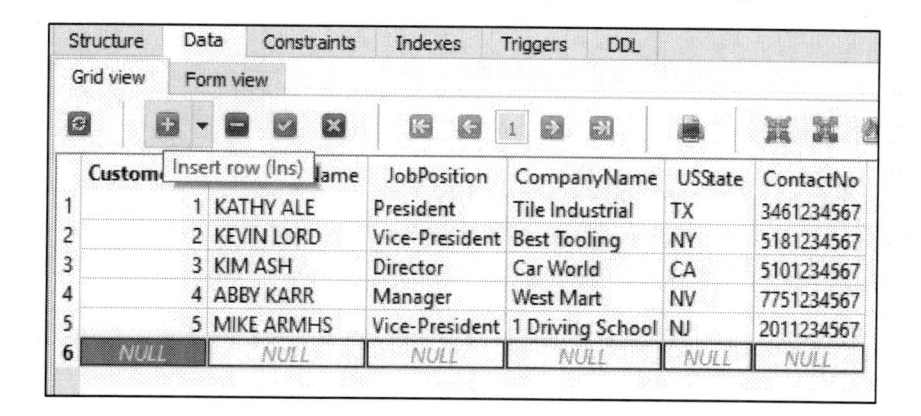

6. Add the following data values in the new record:

   CustomerID: 6
   CustomerName: JOHN DEPP
   JobPosition: President
   CompanyName: Rockers Mine Company
   USState: TX
   ContactNo: 3467654321

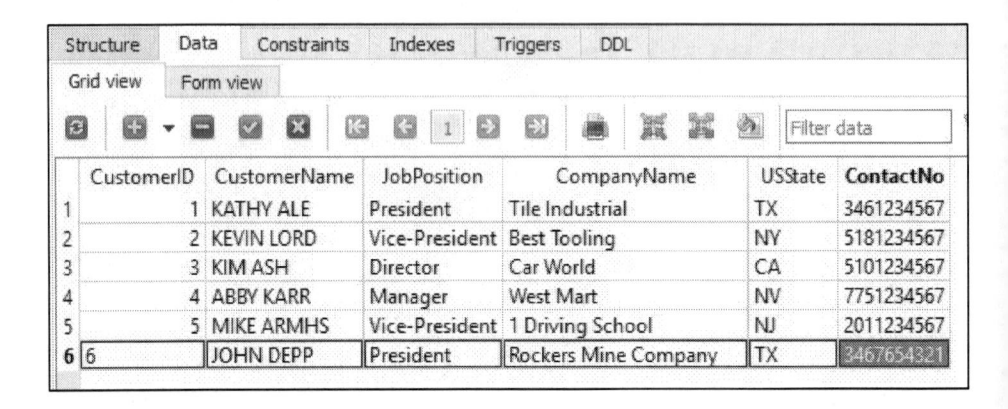

	CustomerID	CustomerName	JobPosition	CompanyName	USState	ContactNo
1	1	KATHY ALE	President	Tile Industrial	TX	3461234567
2	2	KEVIN LORD	Vice-President	Best Tooling	NY	5181234567
3	3	KIM ASH	Director	Car World	CA	5101234567
4	4	ABBY KARR	Manager	West Mart	NV	7751234567
5	5	MIKE ARMHS	Vice-President	1 Driving School	NJ	2011234567
6	6	JOHN DEPP	President	Rockers Mine Company	TX	3467654321

7. Click the COMMIT button to permanently save the new data values added to the table.

ROLLBACK Command

If the COMMIT command saves all the changes to the database, the ROLLBACK command is the reverse, where all the unsaved changes will be discarded. However, you can only undo transactions since the last COMMIT or ROLLBACK statement executed. The standard syntax for this transactional control command is:

ROLLBACK [WORK];

Also, before you can perform a ROLLBACK command, make sure that transactions have started. This means that you need to execute the following programming statement at the very beginning:

BEGIN TRANSACTION;

To demonstrate how a ROLLBACK statement works, you will modify the DROP TABLE command in SQLiteStudio:

1. Click the **SQL editor 1** option. In the QUERY tab, type the following programming statement and click the EXECUTE QUERY button :

   BEGIN TRANSACTION;

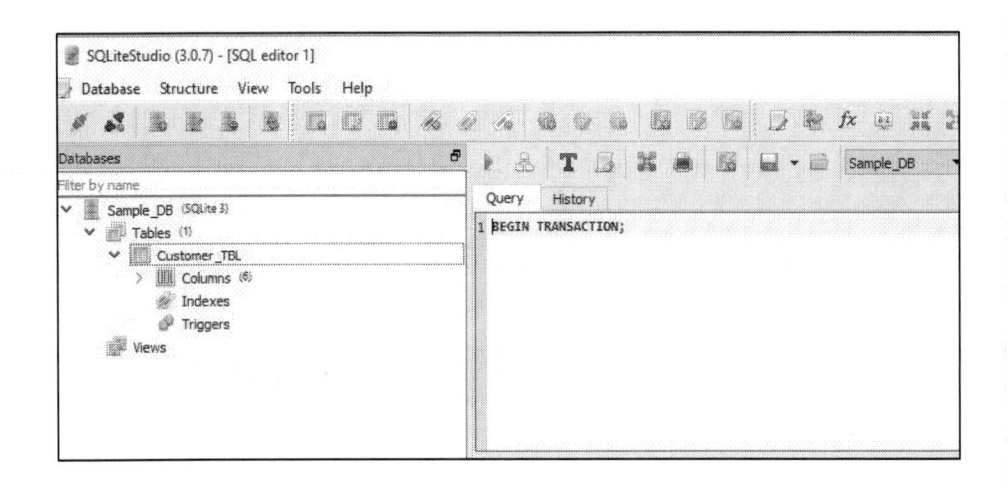

2. Click the **SQL editor 1** option and clear the QUERY tab. Type the following and then click the EXECUTE QUERY button . You will notice that the

124

Customer_TBL table is now removed from the Tables list.

DROP TABLE Customer_TBL;

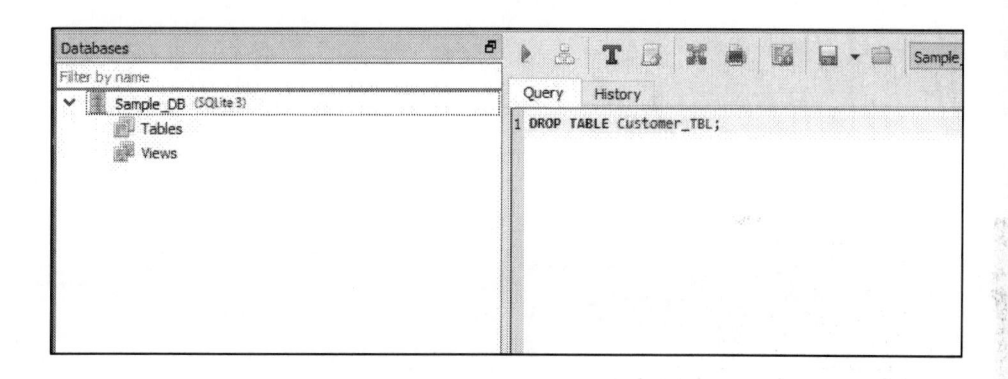

3. Click the **SQL editor 1** option again and clear the QUERY tab. Type the following and then click the EXECUTE QUERY button:

ROLLBACK;

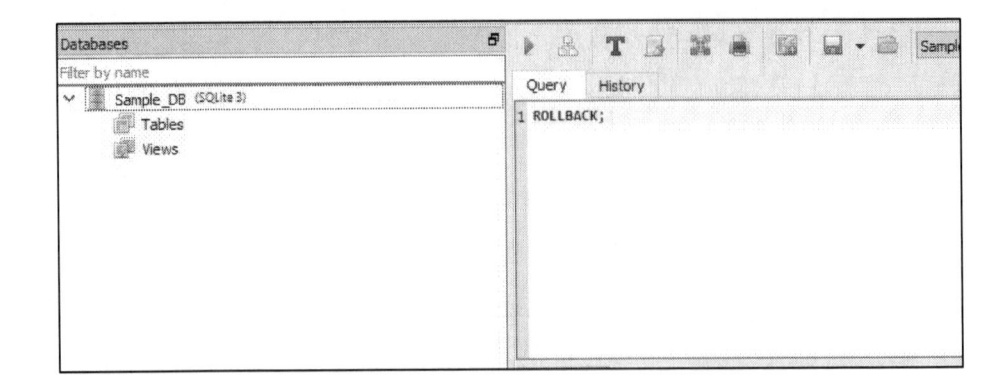

4. To check if the ROLLBACK command reversed the deletion of the **Customer_TBL** table, right-click anywhere inside the DATABASE NAVIGATOR pane. Choose REFRESH ALL DATABASE SCHEMAS option.

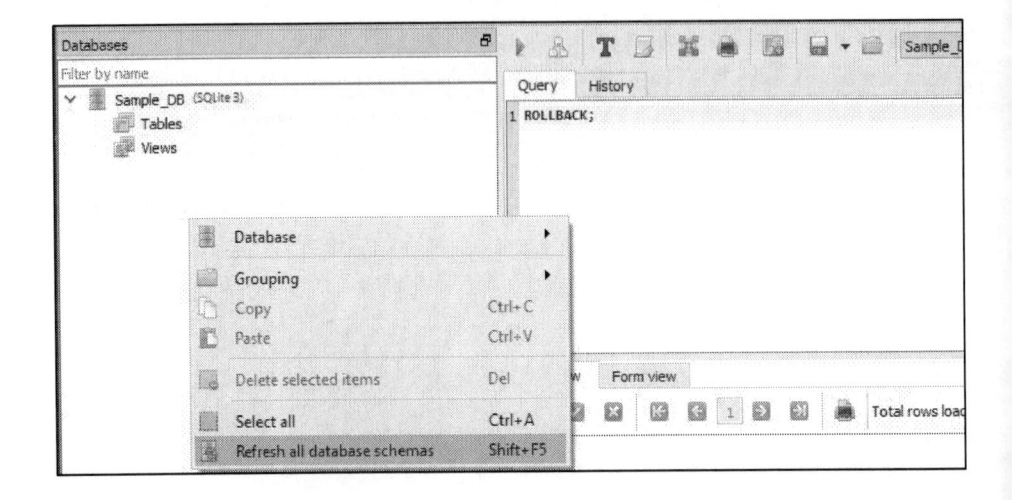

5. Click the TABLE list at the left pane. You should now see that the **Customer_TBL** table is back under the TABLE list.

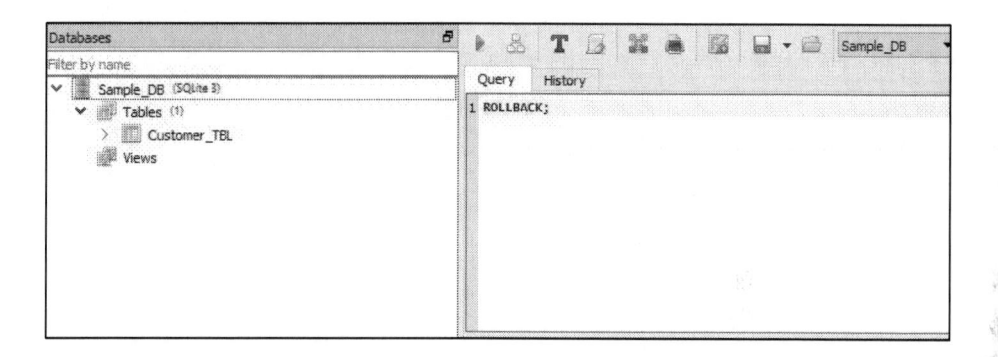

SAVEPOINT Command

When you want to reverse the transaction just back to a certain point and not the entire transaction, then you have to execute the SAVEPOINT command before performing a ROLLBACK action. This is how you manage several transactions into smaller groups of SQL commands. The standard syntax for this transactional control command is:

SAVEPOINT *SAVEPOINT_NAME*;

When using the SAVEPOINT and the ROLLBACK commands together, the syntax is:

ROLLBACK TO *SAVEPOINT_NAME*;

A savepoint name can be the same as the database object's name to which you will be performing the SQL transactions. However, you should remember to make them unique, different from the group of transactions that you want to break down into several points or segments.

To demonstrate how a SAVEPOINT with a ROLLBACK command works, you will delete certain records from the Customer_TBL table and reverse this transaction.

1. Click the **SQL editor 1** option. In the QUERY tab, type the following programming statement and click the EXECUTE QUERY button ▶ :

    BEGIN TRANSACTION;

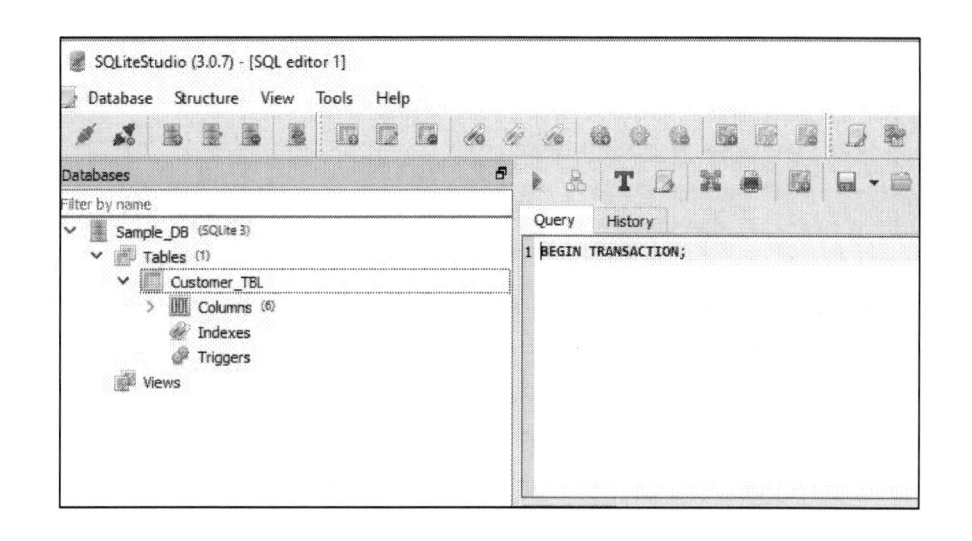

2. Click the **SQL editor 1** option again and clear the QUERY tab. Then type the following:

SAVEPOINT Customer_SP1;

Click the EXECUTE QUERY button. A savepoint section is created before deleting the last record of the **Customer_TBL** table.

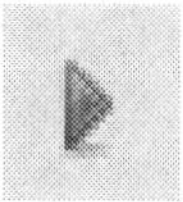

```
1 SAVEPOINT Customer_SP1;
```

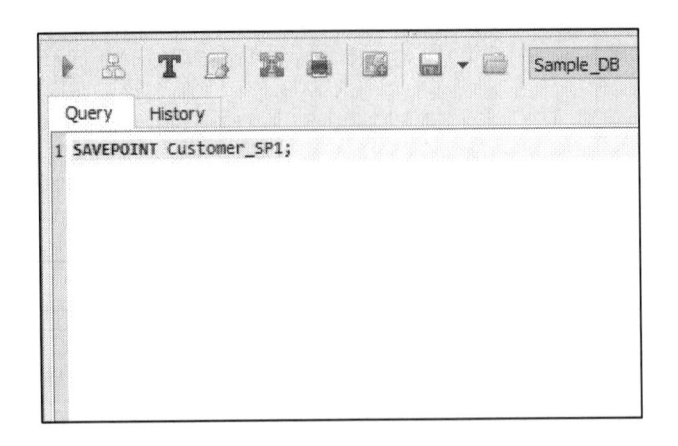

3. To delete the last record of the **Customer_TBL** table, click the SQL editor 1 option and clear the QUERY tab. Type the following and then click the EXECUTE QUERY button :

DELETE FROM Customer_TBL WHERE CustomerID = 6;

```
1 DELETE FROM Customer_TBL WHERE CustomerID = 6;
```

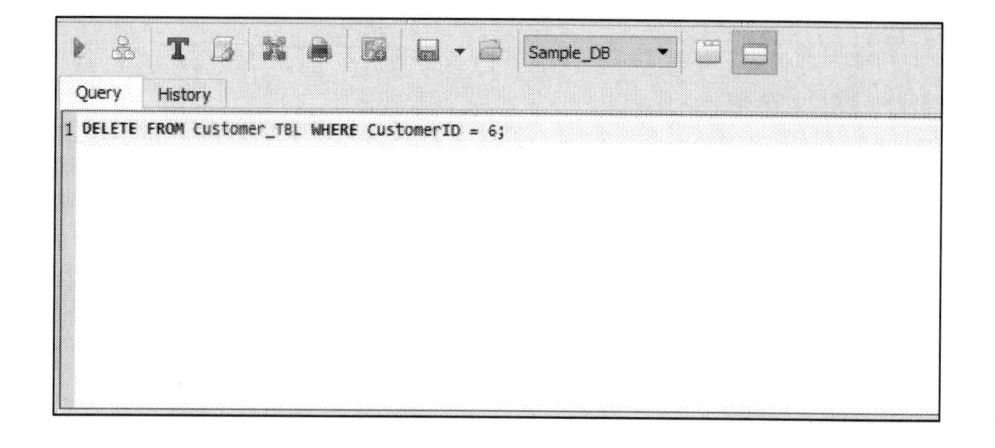

4. To check if the record was deleted, double-click **Customer_TBL** under the TABLES list in the DATABASE NAVIGATOR pane then click the DATA tab at the right. Under the GRID VIEW tab, click the REFRESH TABLE DATA button or press F5 on your keyboard. Your table should be the same as the following:

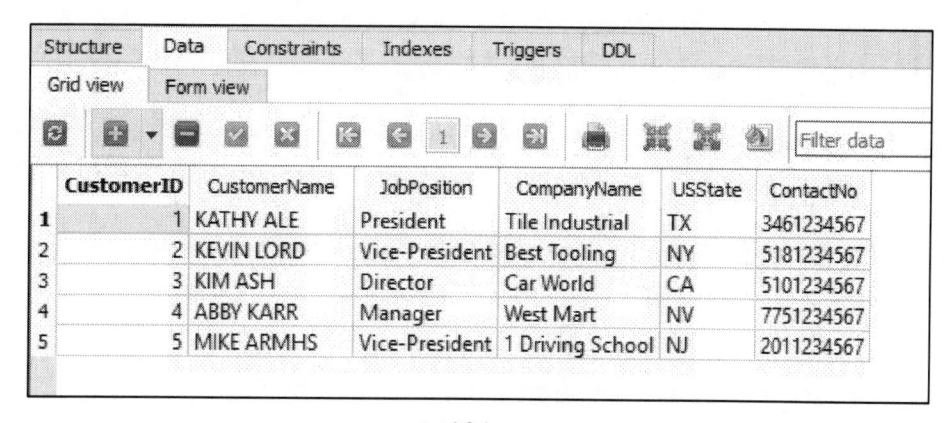

CustomerID	CustomerName	JobPosition	CompanyName	USState	ContactNo
1	KATHY ALE	President	Tile Industrial	TX	3461234567
2	KEVIN LORD	Vice-President	Best Tooling	NY	5181234567
3	KIM ASH	Director	Car World	CA	5101234567
4	ABBY KARR	Manager	West Mart	NV	7751234567
5	MIKE ARMHS	Vice-President	1 Driving School	NJ	2011234567

131

5. To create the second savepoint section, click the **SQL editor 1** option again. Clear the QUERY tab and then type the following:

   SAVEPOINT Customer_SP2;

   Click the EXECUTE QUERY button . This time a savepoint section is created before deleting the record where the **CustomerID** is equal to 5.

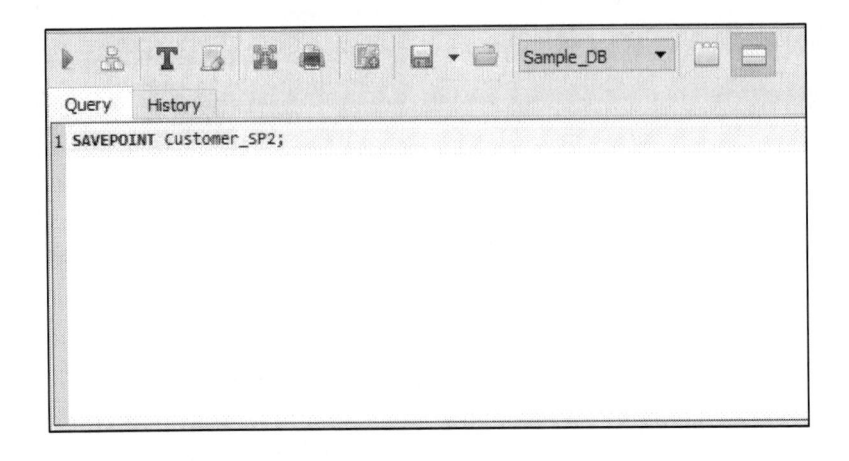

   ```
   1 SAVEPOINT Customer_SP2;
   ```

6. To delete the record where the **CustomerID** is equal to 5, click the SQL editor 1 option again and clear the QUERY tab. Type the following and click the EXECUTE QUERY button :

DELETE FROM Customer_TBL WHERE CustomerID = 5;

```
1 DELETE FROM Customer_TBL WHERE CustomerID = 5;
```

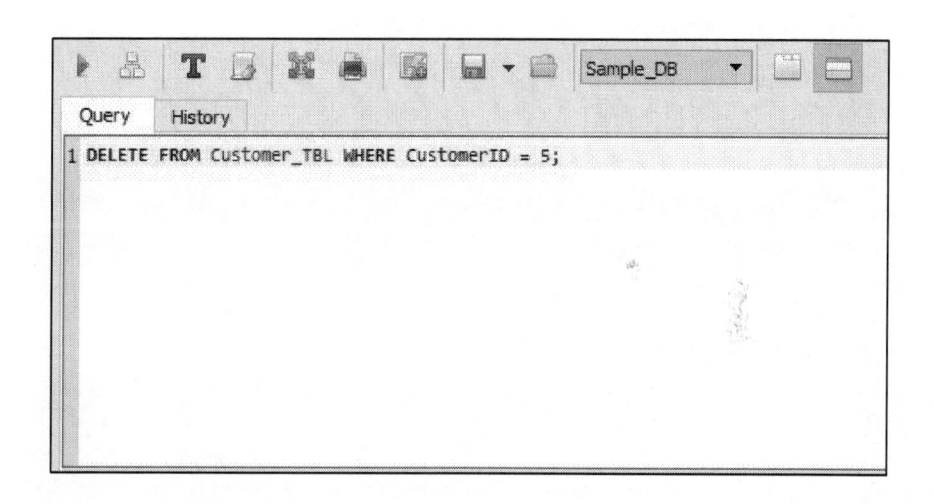

7. To check if the record was deleted, click the Customer_TBL (Sample_DB) option at the bottom left corner of the screen then click the DATA tab at the right. Under the GRID VIEW tab, click the REFRESH

133

TABLE DATA button ![icon] or press F5. Your table should be the same as the following:

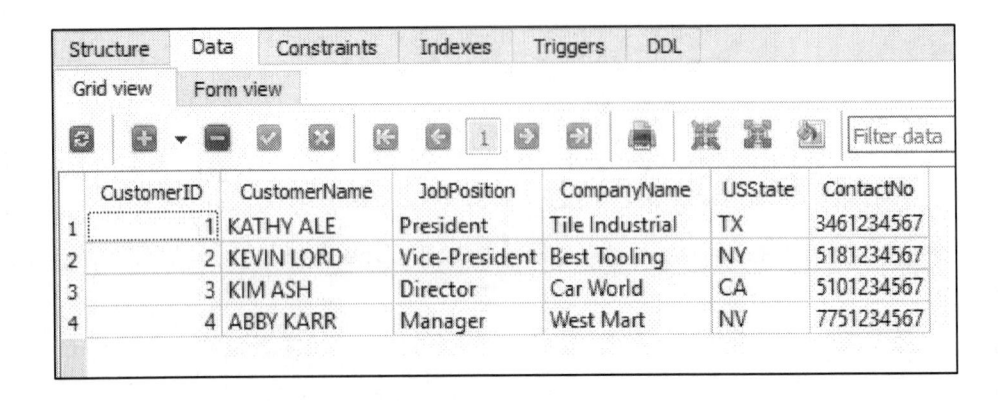

	CustomerID	CustomerName	JobPosition	CompanyName	USState	ContactNo
1	1	KATHY ALE	President	Tile Industrial	TX	3461234567
2	2	KEVIN LORD	Vice-President	Best Tooling	NY	5181234567
3	3	KIM ASH	Director	Car World	CA	5101234567
4	4	ABBY KARR	Manager	West Mart	NV	7751234567

8. To reverse the last transaction done, click the SQL editor 1 option again and clear the QUERY tab. Type the following and then click the EXECUTE QUERY button :

ROLLBACK TO Customer_SP2;

```
1 ROLLBACK TO Customer_SP2;
```

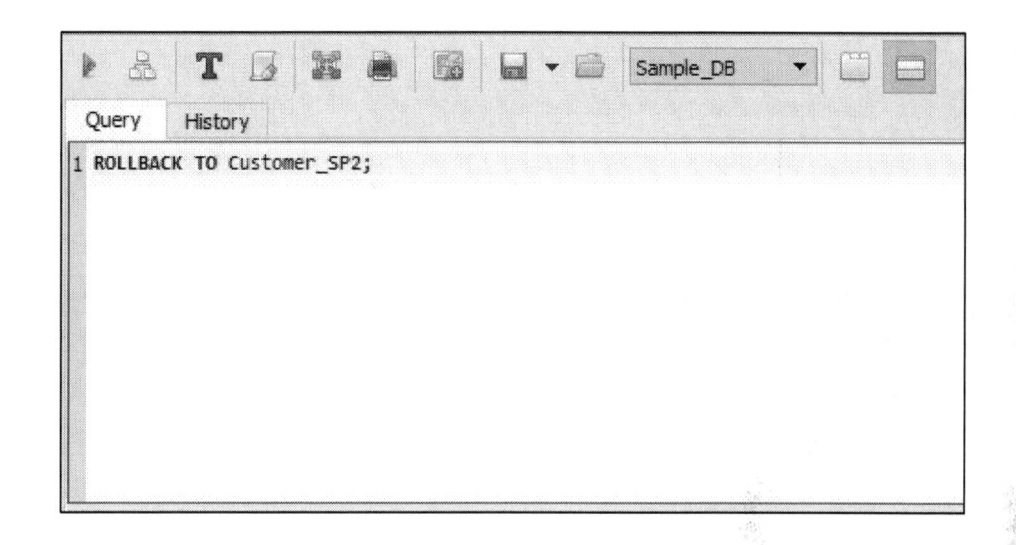

9. To check if the record deletion was reversed, click the Customer_TBL (Sample_DB) option and then click the DATA tab at the right. Under the GRID VIEW tab, click the REFRESH TABLE DATA button or press F5. Your table should be the same as the one below:

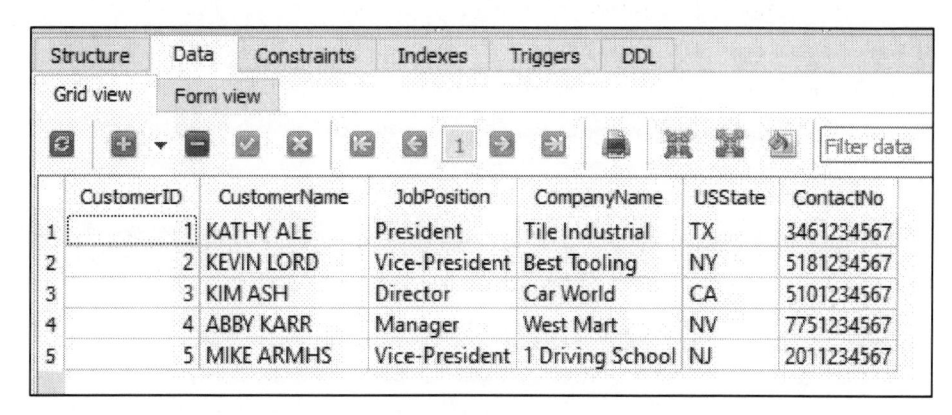

CustomerID	CustomerName	JobPosition	CompanyName	USState	ContactNo
1	KATHY ALE	President	Tile Industrial	TX	3461234567
2	KEVIN LORD	Vice-President	Best Tooling	NY	5181234567
3	KIM ASH	Director	Car World	CA	5101234567
4	ABBY KARR	Manager	West Mart	NV	7751234567
5	MIKE ARMHS	Vice-President	1 Driving School	NJ	2011234567

10. To undo the first record deleted, click the **SQL editor 1** option again and clear the QUERY tab. Type the following and then click the EXECUTE QUERY button :

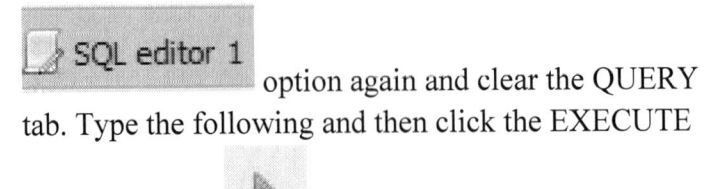

ROLLBACK TO Customer_SP1;

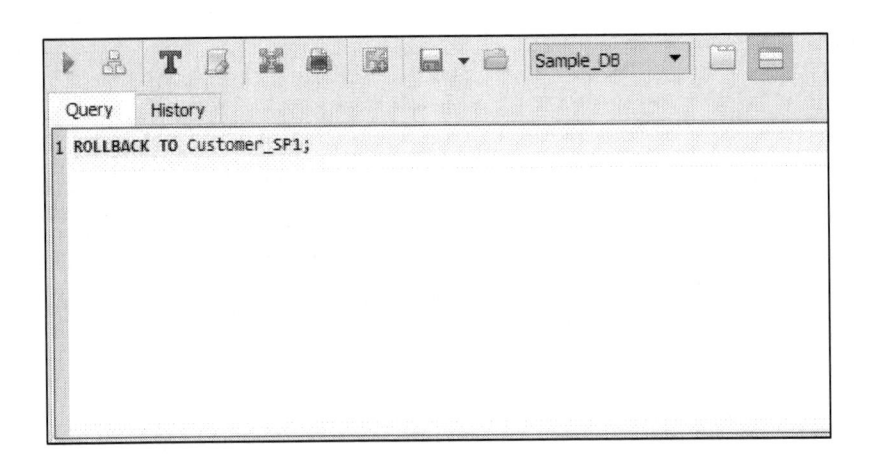

1. To check if the record deletion was reversed, click the **Customer_TBL (Sample_DB)** option, and then click the DATA tab at the right. Under the GRID VIEW tab, click

136

the REFRESH TABLE DATA button ![refresh] or press F5. Your table should be the same as the one below:

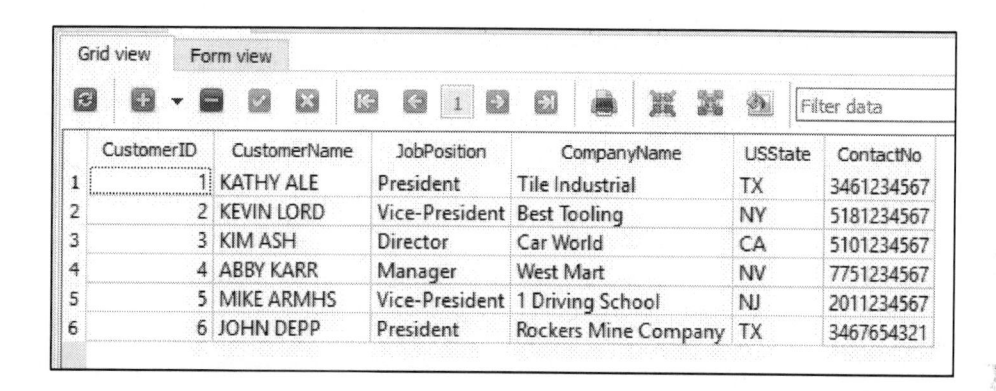

	CustomerID	CustomerName	JobPosition	CompanyName	USState	ContactNo
1	1	KATHY ALE	President	Tile Industrial	TX	3461234567
2	2	KEVIN LORD	Vice-President	Best Tooling	NY	5181234567
3	3	KIM ASH	Director	Car World	CA	5101234567
4	4	ABBY KARR	Manager	West Mart	NV	7751234567
5	5	MIKE ARMHS	Vice-President	1 Driving School	NJ	2011234567
6	6	JOHN DEPP	President	Rockers Mine Company	TX	3467654321

In this chapter, you have learned the primary functions of the three transactional control commands in saving or discarding changes in an SQL database. In the next chapter, you will learn the importance of views and how to manipulate them using CREATE, UPDATE and DROP commands.

137

Chapter Nine: Database Views

In this chapter, you will learn what a database view is and its importance in SQL programming. In addition, you will be able to perform the existing SQL commands in creating, updating and dropping views.

Defining Views

A view is a database object formed when your SELECT queries are saved in the database for future use. This means that a view exists because of the tables where its data values were derived. Thus, one or more tables can create a database view. Also, it has the same characteristics similar to the actual table except that you don't need some physical space to store it (temporarily saved in the computer's memory). Moreover, being a virtual table, you cannot modify its data values.

When executing a SELECT statement to create the view, you can either get the column names from a particular table, or perform certain functions and calculations that will manipulate the given data values. Once created, these views can perform any of the following tasks:

- Simplify data retrieval - Some end users may not have the knowledge to perform database operations to get the query result they need. So, to make things easier, you can create different views from the tables that users require.

- Implement database security – There are times that you have to restrict certain users on what they can access from your database, whether they are allowed to modify data or just view information. To ensure that the tables are secured, you can generate views that only display the data values that you allow users to access.

- Support data summarization and report generation – Through views, you are able to turn a complicated SELECT query into a simple summarized data that you can generate from multiple tables. This summary or report could be generated and updated from time to time. That is why instead of composing complex programming lines you can just use aggregate functions incorporated in the creation of views.

Creating Views

The SQL statement CREATE VIEW is used in generating views from one or more tables, and even from another view. The following is the most basic syntax used in creating a view from a single table:

CREATE VIEW *VIEW_NAME* AS
  SELECT *COLUMN_LIST*
  FROM *TABLE_NAME*;

- **Creating a View from the Entire Content of a Single Table**

    For this exercise, you will be using the Customer_TBL table of the Sample_DB database to create a Customer_VW view in SQLiteStudio.

    1. Click the [SQL editor 1] option and delete everything inside the QUERY tab. Then type the following lines of code:

        CREATE VIEW Customer_VW AS
          SELECT *
          FROM Customer_TBL;

    2. Click the EXECUTE QUERY button [▶] on top of the QUERY tab. You will now notice that there is a Customer_VW view under the VIEWS section, inside the DATABASE NAVIGATOR pane.

140

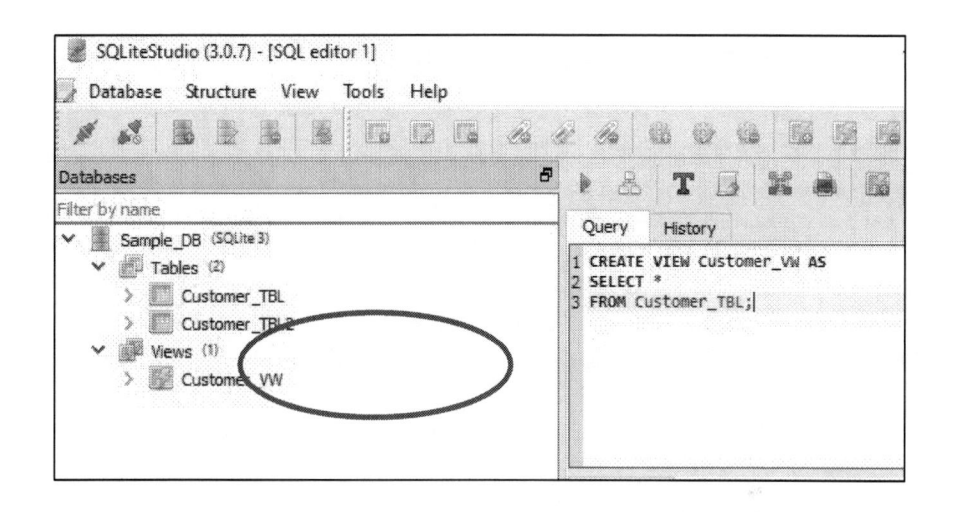

3. To check the content of the view, double-click **Customer_VW** in the left pane then the DATA tab in SQL WORK AREA. The **Customer_VW** view should contain all the records of the **Customer_TBL** table.

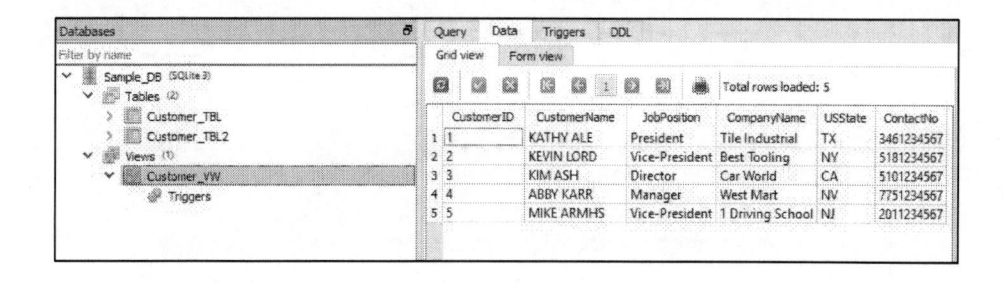

- **Creating a View from Selected Columns of a Single Table**

    If you want to create a view that contains only the contact details of the customer (CustomerName, CompanyName and ContactNo), then you will select certain columns from the Customer_TBL table.

    1. Click the **SQL editor 1** option and delete everything inside the QUERY tab. Then type the following lines of code:

    CREATE VIEW CustContactDeatails_VW AS
      SELECT CustomerName, CompanyName, ContactNo
        FROM Customer_TBL;

    You need to provide a different name for this new view. SQLiteStudio will not allow you to create a new view with the same name as an existing view.

2. Click the EXECUTE QUERY button on top of the QUERY tab. You will now notice that there is a **CustContactDetails_VW** view under the VIEWS section, just on top of the **Customer_VW** view. The VIEWS list is alphabetically arranged in ascending order.

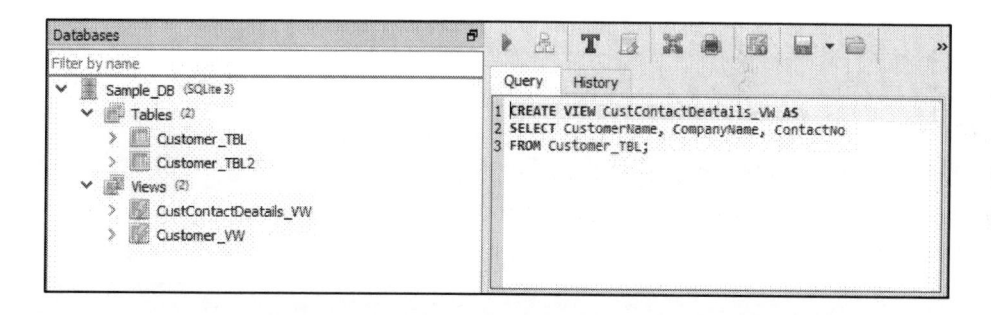

3. To check the content of this newly created view, double-click **CustContactDetails_VW** in the left pane then click the DATA tab again. This view should contain only three columns, namely **CustomerName**, **CompanyName** and **ContactNo**, from the **Customer_TBL** table.

143

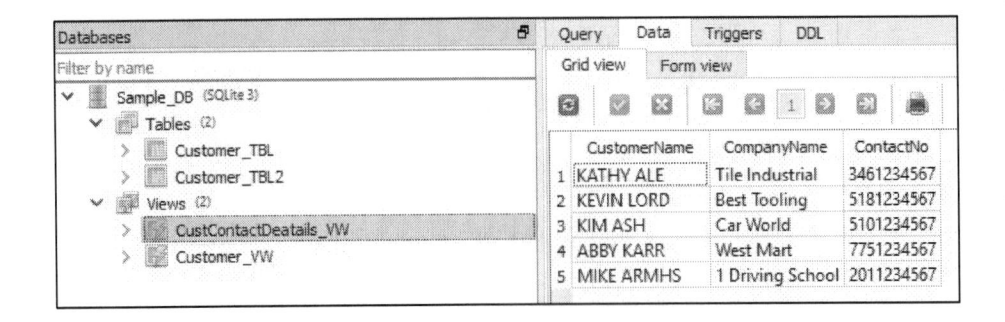

	CustomerName	CompanyName	ContactNo
1	KATHY ALE	Tile Industrial	3461234567
2	KEVIN LORD	Best Tooling	5181234567
3	KIM ASH	Car World	5101234567
4	ABBY KARR	West Mart	7751234567
5	MIKE ARMHS	1 Driving School	2011234567

- **Creating a View from Multiple Tables**

When you require multiple database tables to create the view you need, ensure that the tables involved will have to be joined by columns that are common to them. For example, you may have another table that contains information on the customers' orders such as the date when they ordered, what product they ordered, the quantity and more. This new table will be called the ORDER TABLE and it is related to the first CUSTOMER TABLE because every order is associated to a particular customer.

Now, you will create a view from two tables that will show database users to which company and state each order was shipped to or delivered. The basic syntax for creating a view using multiple tables is:

CREATE VIEW *VIEW_NAME* AS

SELECT *COLUMN_LIST*
FROM *TABLE_LIST*
WHERE *CONDITION*;

To create the ORDER TABLE:

1. Using the data values in Chapter 2 for the **ORDER** table, create another table using the SQL Editor. Click the **SQL editor 1** option and delete everything inside the QUERY tab. Type the following lines of code for the new **ORDER** table:

   CREATE TABLE Order_TBL
        (OrderID INTEGER NOT NULL PRIMARY KEY,
         OrderDate DATE NOT NULL,
         CustomerID INTEGER NOT NULL,
         ProductID INTEGER NOT NULL,
         OrderQty BIGINTEGER NOT NULL);

2. Click the EXECUTE QUERY button on top of the QUERY tab. You will now have the **Order_TBL** table under the TABLES list in the left pane.

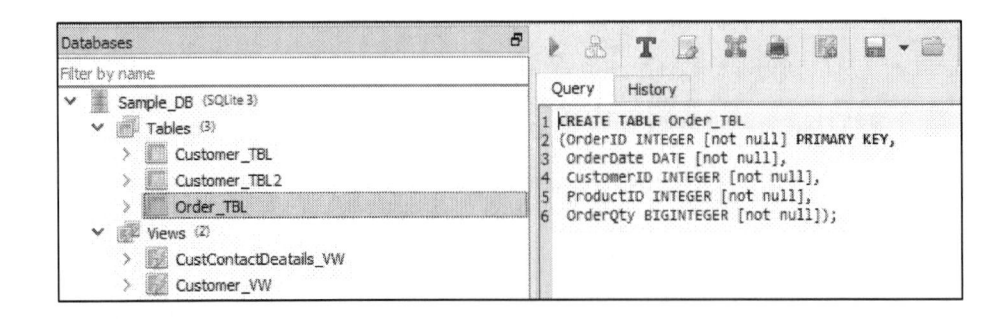

3. Double-click the **Order_TBL** in the left pane then click on DATA tab at the left. You will populate this table with data values in GRID VIEW mode.

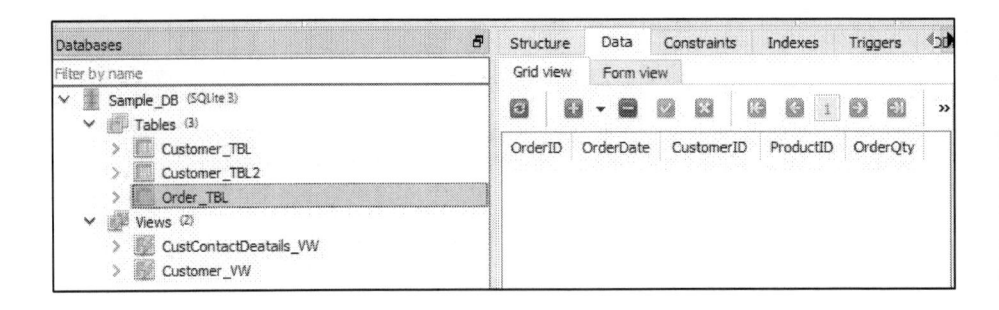

4. Click the INSERT ROW button and then select the first option – INSERT MULTIPLE ROWS.

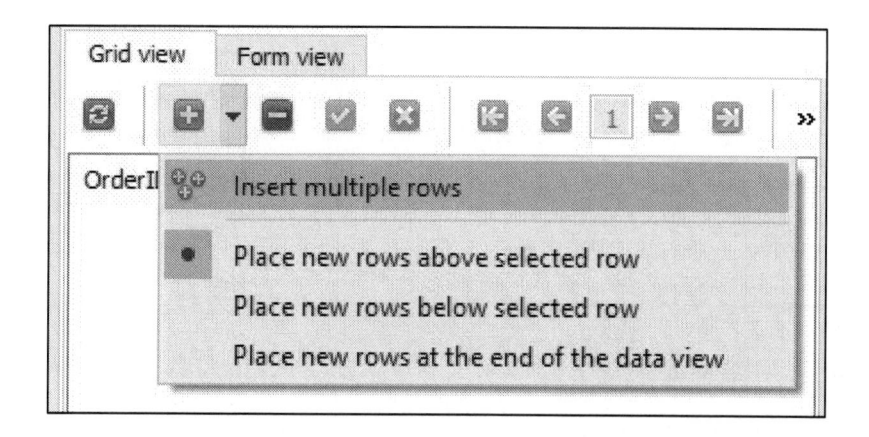

5. Enter "4" in the NUMBER OF ROWS TO INSERT input box (since there are 4 records in the ORDER TABLE from Chapter 2) then click OK.

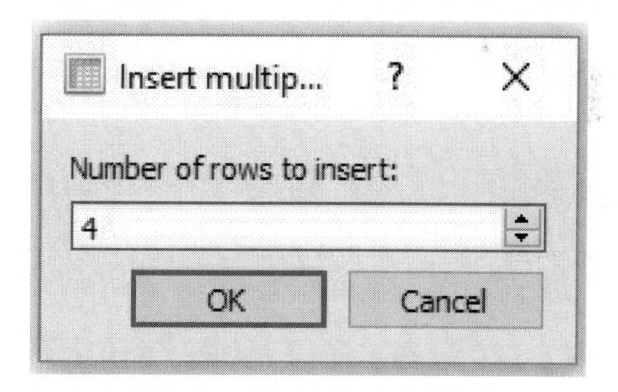

6. The **Order_TBL** table will now have 4 rows and 5 columns. Instead of using SQL statements to populate this table, you will enter

147

the values directly into the table (check the data values in Chapter 2).

	OrderID	OrderDate	CustomerID	ProductID	OrderQty
1	1	2016-05-23	1	4	300
2	2	2016-09-09	1	5	100
3	3	2016-02-17	3	2	150
4	4	2016-05-12	2	2	500

7. Click the COMMIT button to save all the data values of the **Order_TBL** table.

To create the view that will tell you to which company and state every order was shipped to or delivered:

1. Click the **SQL editor 1** option, empty QUERY tab and then type the following lines of code:

148

```
CREATE VIEW OrderDelivery_VW AS
    SELECT Order_TBL.OrderID,
    Customer_TBL.CompanyName AS
    CompanyDeliveredTo,
    Customer_TBL.USState AS
    StateDestination, Order_TBL.OrderQty
    FROM Customer_TBL, Order_TBL
    WHERE Order_TBL.CustomerID =
Customer_TBL.CustomerID;
```

2. Click the EXECUTE QUERY button on top of the QUERY tab. You will now have a new view named **OrderDelivery_VW**.

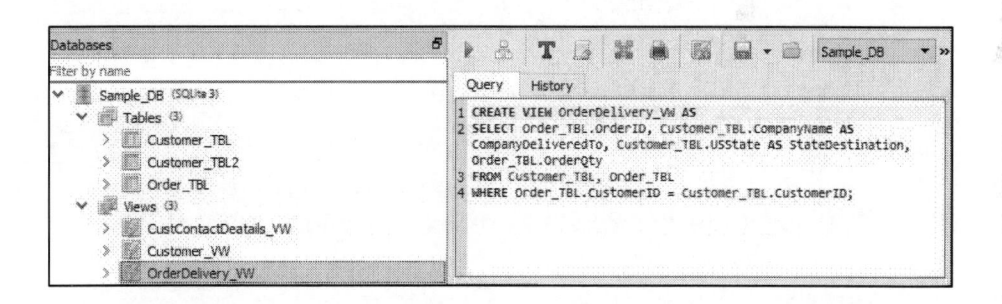

3. To check the content of this view, double-click **OrderDelivery_VW** in the left pane then click the DATA tab at the right.

149

	OrderID	CompanyDeliveredTo	StateDestination	OrderQty
1	1	Tile Industrial	TX	300
2	2	Tile Industrial	TX	100
3	3	Car World	CA	150
4	4	Best Tooling	NY	500

In this view, two columns were selected and renamed from the **Customer_TBL** table - **CompanyName** changed to **CompanyDeliveredTo** and **USState** changed to **StateDestination**. The other two were from **Order_TBL** table- **OrderID** and **OrderQty** (the original column names were retained). The rows retrieved from both tables are those records where the CustomerID of the **Customer_TBL** table matches the CustomerID of the **Order_TBL** table.

Dropping Views

The DROP VIEW command is the statement used to destroy an existing view from the database. The basic syntax is:

DROP VIEW *VIEW_NAME;*

To drop or delete the entire Customer_VW view:

1. Click the **SQL editor 1** option, empty QUERY tab and then type the following lines of code:

   DROP VIEW Customer_VW;

2. Click the EXECUTE QUERY button ▶ on top of the QUERY tab. You will notice that the **Customer_VW** view is already deleted from the Views list.

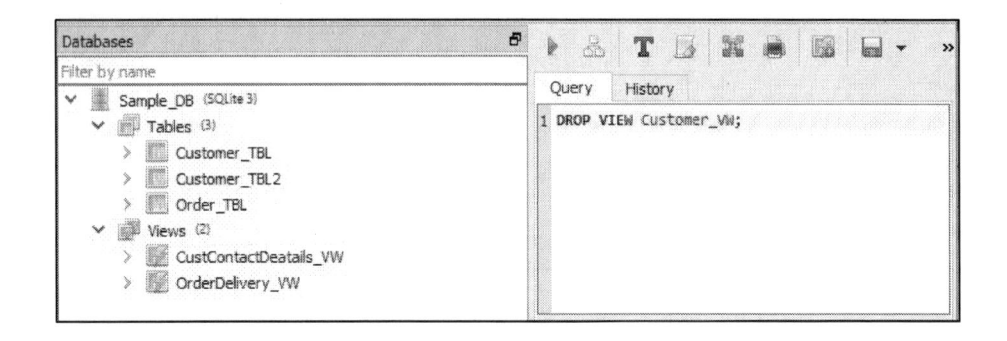

In this chapter, you have learned the definition and importance of database views in SQL. You have also performed common operations in manipulating views, such as creating and dropping them. In the next chapter, you will learn more in-depth concepts in designing databases in SQL – primary and foreign keys, indexes and normalized databases.

Chapter Ten: Enhancing Database Designs

In this chapter, you will gain more in-depth knowledge on enhancing database designs with the use of primary and foreign keys, indexes and normalization techniques. Having a better understanding of designing databases will provide the software application you are using an edge, by performing queries more effectively and maintaining data integrity at all times.

Assigning Primary and Foreign Keys

It is one of the best practices to assign a primary key when you define a database table. In a relational database, the primary key is a special field or combination of fields that make each record in the table unique. Since the presence of the primary key does not permit the duplication of values on the column to which it was assigned, then data integrity is guaranteed. Also, fields that are designated as primary keys cannot contain null values. Defining a primary key, whether it is explicit or implied, occurs during table creation. Normally, the tables with primary keys are regarded as parent tables, meaning these tables provide information to another table or what is termed as the child table. Consequently, child tables are dependent on the parent table.

In the previous chapters, you have been dealing with the CUSTOMER table and the ORDER Table. What if you have another table called the PRODUCT Table that contains the following fields or columns: Product ID, Product Name and Price per Unit? You will have the following relationship from these three tables:

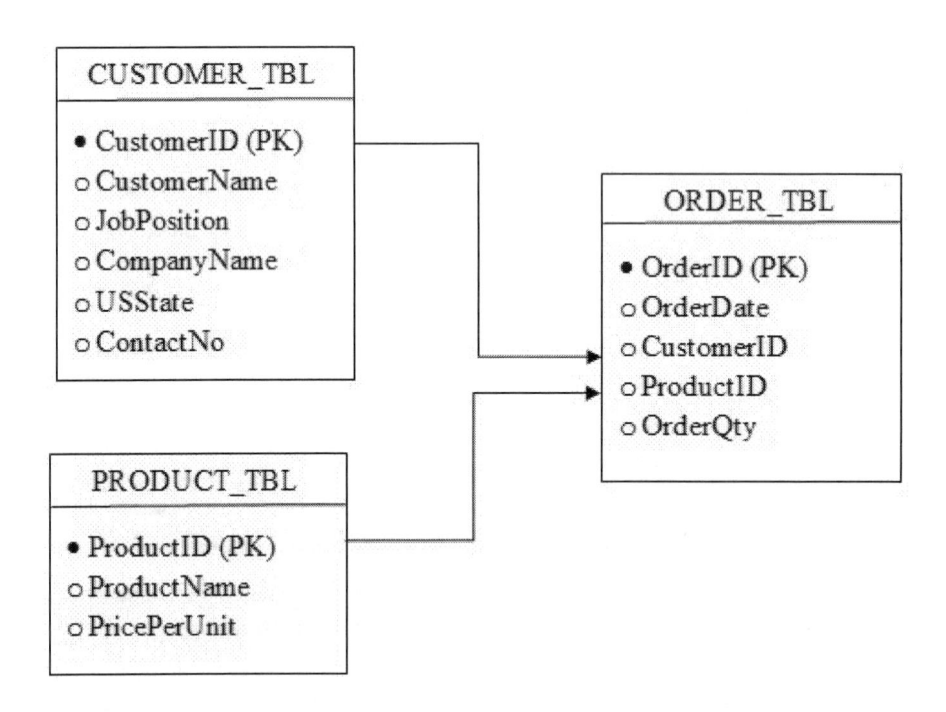

CUSTOMER_TBL
- CustomerID (PK)
  - CustomerName
  - JobPosition
  - CompanyName
  - USState
  - ContactNo

ORDER_TBL
- OrderID (PK)
  - OrderDate
  - CustomerID
  - ProductID
  - OrderQty

PRODUCT_TBL
- ProductID (PK)
  - ProductName
  - PricePerUnit

From the figure above, the CUSTOMER_TBL and the PRODUCT_TBL are the parent tables of the child table ORDER_TBL (this describes a parent-child relationship in database design). As you can see, the fields named CustomerID and ProductID are the primary keys of the parent tables. These two fields are also present in the child table. They now become foreign keys of the ORDER_TBL table. In other words, a foreign key is a column or field present in the child table that references to the primary key of its parent table.

Unlike the primary key, a foreign key does not need to be unique all the time. In addition, the name of the foreign key could be different from the name of the primary key that it references to. Furthermore, the ProductID of the parent table (PRODUCT_TBL) can never have duplicate entries, but not the corresponding ProductID in the child table (ORDER_TBL). However, you should not define and create a foreign key value if there is no matching primary key value.

Understanding Indexes

When a database starts to slow down, specifically its SQL queries, you can create and implement indexes to improve its performance. Such indexes are important objects that serve as pointers associated to the data of a particular table. The primary function of an index is to determine the exact physical location of the data when a query is executed to improve its retrieval process. It works like a book's alphabetically arranged index that helps you find the information you need in a much easier way using its page numbers. Thus, time is saved, since you do not need to scan one row at a time (most especially in extremely large databases) and just go directly to the required record.

The storage spaces of an index and the table from which it was created are separate. Such allocated physical space can also increase tremendously, even larger than the table it references. That is why storage requirements are taken into consideration when designing databases. Just like tables and views, indexes can also be created or dropped. When designed correctly, they actually speed up SELECT queries but could slow down DELETE, UPDATE and INSERT statements. For enormous databases, data retrieval will definitely consume much time. However, such index transactions have no effect on the table's data.

- **Creating Indexes**

An index is associated to a particular column when it is created. It then holds the location of the data values of the table that contains that particular indexed column. Whenever new data is added to the table, it will also be added to the index. Let's say you execute a SELECT statement with a certain condition specified in the WHERE clause that checks the column that is indexed. The first thing that will happen is that the index is first searched and will only return the exact location if the data value is found.

For example, you wanted to select all the records from the ORDER table where the Customer ID matches to 1. You will then issue the following query:

SELECT *
FROM Order_TBL
WHERE CustomerID = 1;

If the ORDER_TBL table is indexed on the CustomerID column, then the records will be arranged in an ascending order based on that column. Thus, the CustomerID index makes it easier for the search process to take place and finally resolves the location of all the data with the matching Customer ID. Once the location is determined, the corresponding rows of data will be retrieved from the ORDER_TBL table. Without the existence of the index, a full scan will be performed, which will not be efficient if the table contains hundreds or even thousands of records.

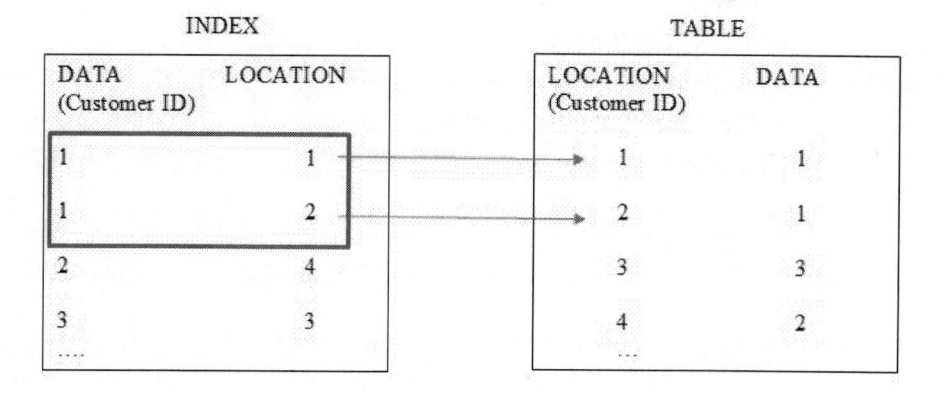

INDEX		TABLE	
DATA (Customer ID)	LOCATION	LOCATION (Customer ID)	DATA
1	1	1	1
1	2	2	1
2	4	3	3
3	3	4	2
....		...	

The basic syntax is for creating an index is:

CREATE INDEX *INDEX_NAME* ON *TABLE_NAME* [(*COLUMN_NAME*)];

This statement can vary by adding specifications such as the column name to be indexed, ordering (whether ascending or descending) and many more. Now, to create the ColumnID index of the ORDER_TBL table in SQLiteStudio:

1. Click the **SQL editor 1** option and make sure the QUERY tab is empty. Then type the following:

CREATE INDEX CustomerID_IDX ON Order_TBL (CustomerID);

```
1 CREATE INDEX CustomerID_IDX ON Order_TBL (CustomerID);
```

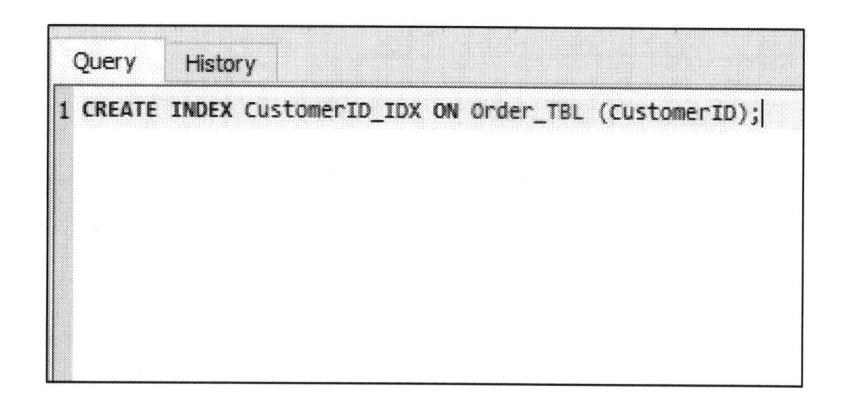

2. Click the EXECUTE QUERY button on top of the QUERY tab. You will now have **CustomerID_IDX** under the INDEXES list in the **Order_TBL** table.

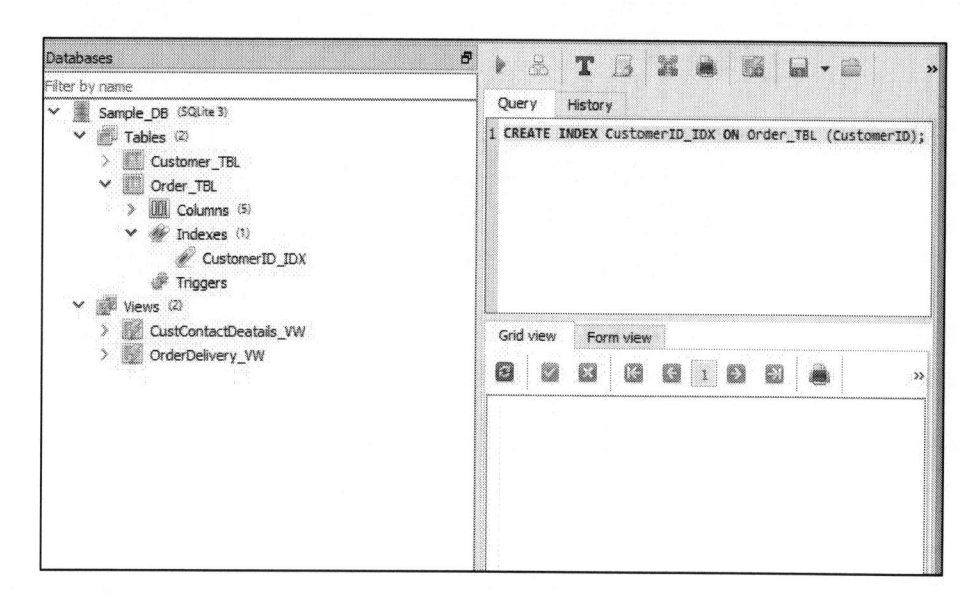

- **Dropping Indexes**

    Just like dropping a table or a view, you will use the following basic syntax:

    DROP INDEX *INDEX_NAME*;

    Remember that you can re-create the index after it has been deleted, but make sure you take extra precaution when performing such transactions. Also, when you delete a table, you will also be deleting all the corresponding indexes with it. Sometimes you may only need to delete the index and retain the table. Such implementation happens when you only want to fix an index problem to optimize the database performance and reduce fragmentation.

    To drop the index that we have created previously:

    1. Click the [SQL editor 1] option and make sure the QUERY tab is empty. Then type the following:

DROP INDEX CustomerID_IDX;

```
Query   History
1 DROP INDEX CustomerID_IDX;
```

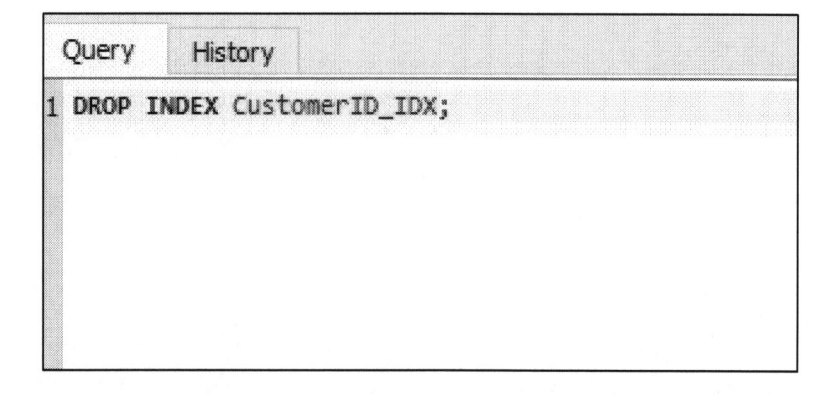

2. Click the EXECUTE QUERY button on top of the QUERY tab. You will now notice that the **CustomerID_IDX** index has been deleted from the Indexes list.

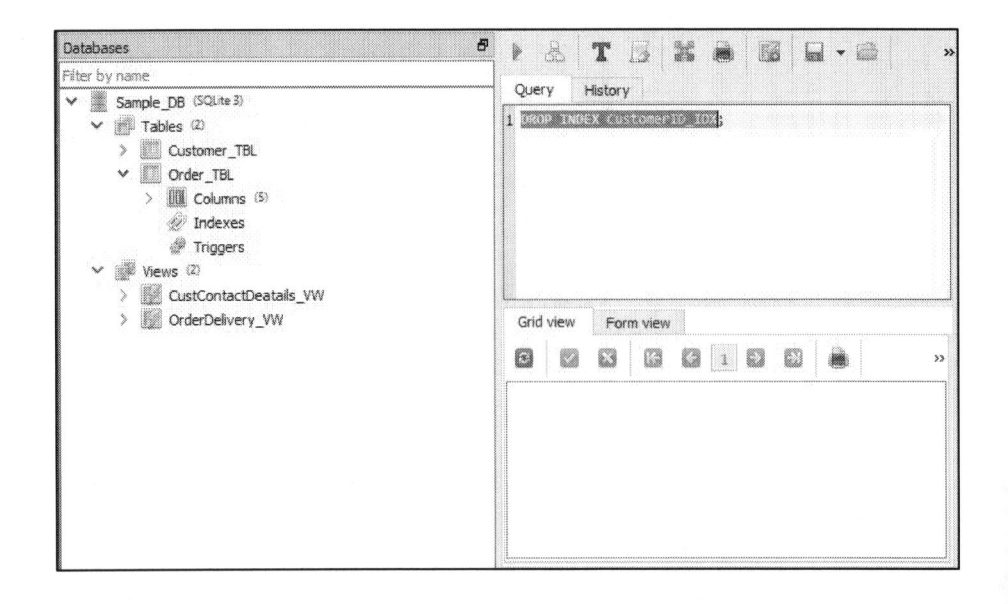

Normalizing Databases

Why do you need to normalize a database? This is because in designing a database you need to ensure that information is well organized, easily managed, always accurate and there is no unnecessary duplication. Basically, normalization is the process of designing and redesigning a database by reducing one big table into two smaller tables, where the same type of data are grouped together. For example, if you only have one table by merging the customer information of the CUSTOMER_TBL table with the ORDER_TBL table, then you will get a table that is not normalized:

ORDER ID	ORDER DATE	CUSTOMER ID	NAME	POSITION	COMPANY	STATE	CONTACT NO	PRODUCT ID	ORDER QTY
1	2016-05-23	1	Kathy Ale	President	Tile Industrial	TX	3461234567	4	300
2	2016-09-09	1	Kathy Ale	President	Tile Industrial	TX	3461234567	5	100
3	2016-02-17	3	Kim Ash	Director	Car World	CA	5101234567	2	150
4	2016-05-12	2	Kevin Lord	VP	Best Tooling	NY	5181234567	2	500

As you can see, there is a redundancy of data on the part of storing the customer information. That is why it is way better to divide this table into two smaller ones through the normalization process. Always bear in mind to keep data redundancy to a minimum, if possible, to save storage space and avoid information confusion. If you have customer information for every table and one table does not match such information with another, then how will you be able to verify which one is correct? If you have to update a customer address, then you are required to update the data in all of the tables where it is included. Thus, time and effort in managing the database is wasted.

The way of measuring the depth or level to which a database has been normalized is called a normal form. There are three common normal forms, where each form is dependent on the previous normalization steps performed on the database.

- **First Normal Form (1NF)**

Given a set of base data, the first normal form (1NF) aims to divide this into logical units or tables of related information with an assigned primary key. Every cell contained in any of the 2-dimensional tables should only have a single value. Each row of a particular table refers to a certain record of information and must always be unique. As for the column, it is given a unique name and consists of data values of the same type, which pertains to a single attribute of the information contained in the table. Moreover, there is no particular order that the columns nor the rows should be arranged.

Modifying the given database in Chapter 2 by adding employee information, you will have the following base data for the company:

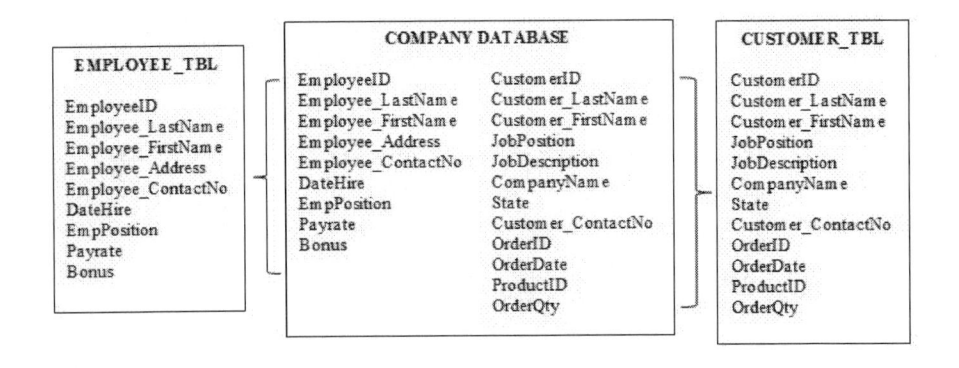

```
      EMPLOYEE_TBL              COMPANY DATABASE                CUSTOMER_TBL

  EmployeeID              EmployeeID         CustomerID          CustomerID
  Employee_LastName       Employee_LastName  Customer_LastName   Customer_LastName
  Employee_FirstName      Employee_FirstName Customer_FirstName  Customer_FirstName
  Employee_Address        Employee_Address   JobPosition         JobPosition
  Employee_ContactNo      Employee_ContactNo JobDescription      JobDescription
  DateHire                DateHire           CompanyName         CompanyName
  EmpPosition             EmpPosition        State               State
  Payrate                 Payrate            Customer_ContactNo  Customer_ContactNo
  Bonus                   Bonus              OrderID             OrderID
                                             OrderDate           OrderDate
                                             ProductID           ProductID
                                             OrderQty            OrderQty
```

Based from the figure above, the entire company database was divided into two smaller tables – EMPLOYEE_TBL and CUSTOMER_TBL. The primary key for these tables are EmployeeID and CustomerID respectively. In this way, it is easier to read and manage the information as compared to one big table with so many columns and rows. The data values stored in each table refer to two separate entities, meaning those pieces of information describing the company's employees are only present in the EMPLOYEE_TBL table while those that only pertain to the customers are stored in the CUSTOMER_TBL table.

- **Second Normal Form (2NF)**

After you are done with the first normal form, the next step is deriving the second normal form (2NF). This process focuses on functional dependency that describes the relationships between attributes. When an attribute determines the value of another, then there is functional dependency between them. In this case, you will store data values from the Employee and Customer tables that are partly dependent on their primary keys into separate tables.

```
EMPLOYEE_TBL                          EMPLOYEE_TBL

EmployeeID                            EmployeeID
Employee_LastName                     Employee_LastName
Employee_FirstName                    Employee_FirstName
Employee_Address                      Employee_Address
Employee_ContactNo                    Employee_ContactNo
DateHire
EmpPosition
Payrate                               EMPLOYEE_SALARY_TBL
Bonus
                                      EmployeeID
                                      EmpPosition
                                      Payrate
                                      Bonus
```

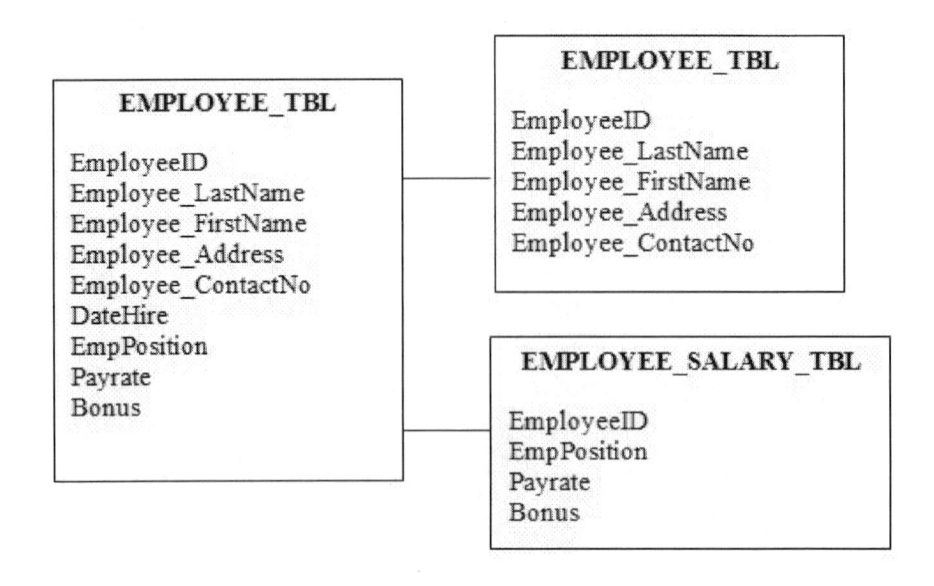

The figure above shows that those attributes that are partly dependent on the EmployeeID primary key have been removed from EMPLOYEE_TBL and stored in a new table called EMPLOYEE_SALARY_TBL. The attributes that were retained in the original table are fully dependent on the primary key – meaning that for every record of last name, first name, address and contract number there is a corresponding particular employee ID. Unlike the EMPLOYEE_SALARY_TBL, a particular employee ID does not reference a unique employee position nor salary rate. There could be more than one employee with the same position (EmpPosition), pay rate (Payrate) and bonus (Bonus).

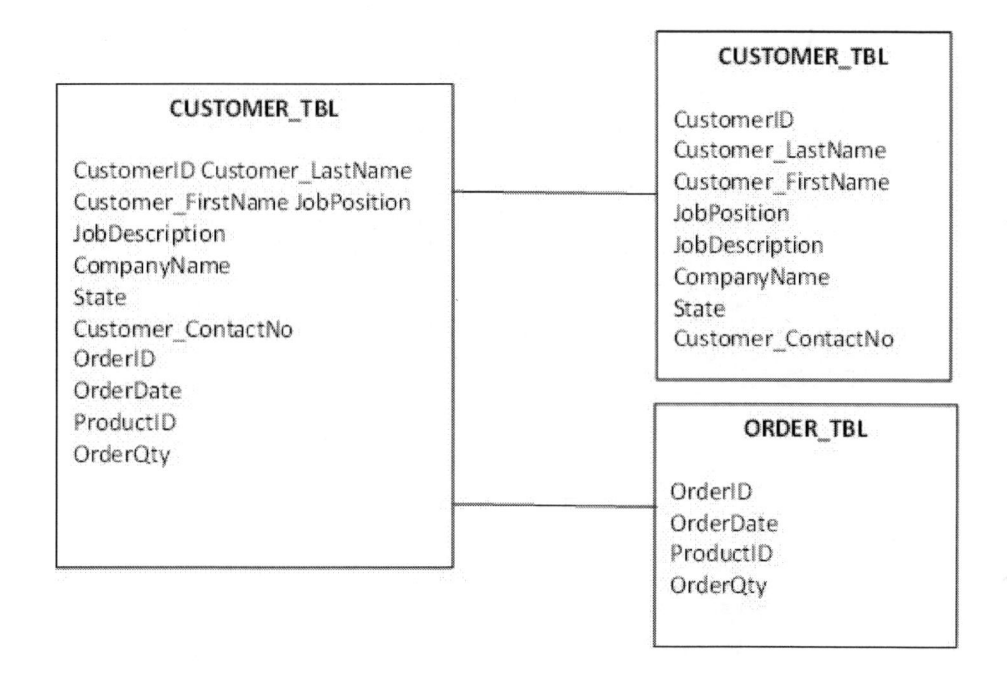

CUSTOMER_TBL

CustomerID Customer_LastName
Customer_FirstName JobPosition
JobDescription
CompanyName
State
Customer_ContactNo
OrderID
OrderDate
ProductID
OrderQty

CUSTOMER_TBL

CustomerID
Customer_LastName
Customer_FirstName
JobPosition
JobDescription
CompanyName
State
Customer_ContactNo

ORDER_TBL

OrderID
OrderDate
ProductID
OrderQty

For the CUSTOMER_TBL table, customer's order information does not directly depend on the general customer information found in the original table. That is why four attributes (OrderID, OrderDate, ProductID and OrderQty) were moved to a separate table called ORDER_TBL.

- **Third Normal Form (3NF)**

With the third normal form (3NF), you will have to separate pieces of information from the table that are completely not dependent on the primary key. Going back to the CUSTOMER_TBL, the job position (JobPosition) and its description (JobDescription) are totally independent of the CustomerID primary key. This is because, in general, any job position will have the same duties and responsibilities regardless of who the customer is. Thus, we will separate the JobPosition and JobDescription attributes into another table called POSITION_TBL.

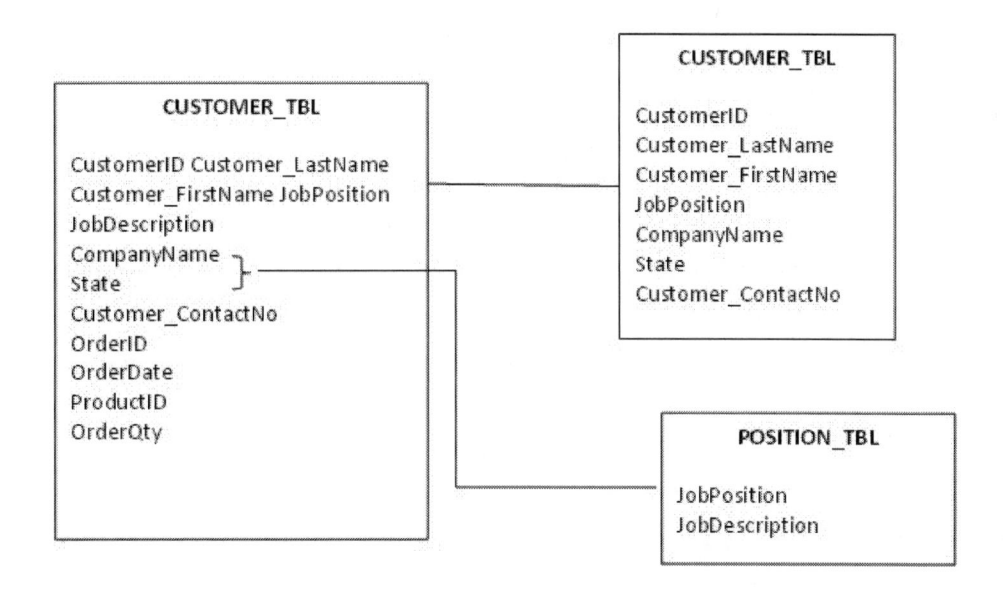

```
CUSTOMER_TBL

CustomerID Customer_LastName
Customer_FirstName JobPosition
JobDescription
CompanyName
State
Customer_ContactNo
OrderID
OrderDate
ProductID
OrderQty
```

```
CUSTOMER_TBL

CustomerID
Customer_LastName
Customer_FirstName
JobPosition
CompanyName
State
Customer_ContactNo
```

```
POSITION_TBL

JobPosition
JobDescription
```

In this chapter, you have learned that there are design practices that you can apply to boost the performance of your databases. Duplicate data values are avoided by assigning primary and foreign keys in tables. Search queries are heightened through the implementation of table indexes. Data consistency and security are improved because of the normalization process. Thus, overall database organization is enhanced. In the next chapter, you will learn some advance topics in SQL design that includes cursors, triggers and errors.

Chapter Eleven: Database Advanced Topics

In this chapter, you will be introduced to some advanced topics in SQL that goes beyond basic database transactions. Even if this section only includes an overview of cursors, triggers and errors, such knowledge could possibly help you extend the features of your SQL implementations.

Cursors

Generally, SQL commands manipulate database objects using set-based operations. This means that transactions are performed on a group or block of data. A cursor, on the other hand, processes data from a table one row at a time. It is created using a compound a statement and destroyed upon exit. The standard syntax for declaring a cursor is (which may differ for every implementation):

DECLARE CURSOR *CURSOR_NAME*
IS {*SELECT_STATEMENT*}

You can perform operations on a cursor only after it has been declared or defined.

- **Open a Cursor**

    Once declared, you perform an OPEN operation to access the cursor and then execute the specified SELECT statement. The results of the SELECT query will be saved in a certain area in the memory. The standard syntax for opening a cursor is:

    OPEN *CURSOR_NAME*;

- **Fetch Data from a Cursor**

    The FETCH statement is performed if you want to retrieve the query results or the data from the cursor. The standard syntax for fetching data is:

    FETCH NEXT FROM *CURSOR_NAME* [INTO *FETCH_LIST*]

    In SQL programming, the optional statement inside the square brackets will let you assign the data retrieved into a certain variable.

- **Close a Cursor**

There is a corresponding CLOSE statement to be executed when you open a particular cursor. Once the cursor is closed, all the names and resources used will be deallocated. Thus, the cursor is no longer available for the program to use. The standard syntax for closing a cursor is:

CLOSE *CURSOR_NAME*

Triggers

There are instances when you want certain SQL operations or transactions to occur after performing some specific actions. This scenario describes an SQL statement that triggers another SQL statement to take place. Essentially, a trigger is an SQL procedure that is compiled in the database that execute certain transactions based on other transactions that have previously occurred. Such triggers can be performed before or after the execution of DML statements (INSERT, DELETE and UPDATE). In addition, triggers can validate data integrity, maintain data consistency, undo transactions, log operations, modify and read data values in different databases.

- **Create a Trigger**

    The standard syntax for creating a trigger is:

    CREATE TRIGGER *TRIGGER_NAME*
    TRIGGER_ACTION_TIMETRIGGER_EVENT

    ON *TABLE_NAME*
    [REFERENCING
    OLD_OR_NEW_VALUE_ALIAS_LIST]
    TRIGGERED_ACTION

    TRIGGER_NAME - the unique identifying name for this object

    TRIGGER_ACTION_TIMETRIGGER_EVENT - the specified time that the set of triggered actions will occur (whether before or after the triggering event).

    TABLE_NAME – the table for which the DML statements have been specified

    TRIGGERED_ACTION – specifies the actions to be performed once an event is triggered

Once a trigger has been created, it cannot be altered anymore. You can just either re-create or replace it. How a trigger works depends what conditions you specify – whether it will fire at once when a DML statement is performed or it will fire multiple times for every table row affected by the DML statement. You can also include a threshold value or a Boolean condition, that when such condition is met will trigger a course of action.

- **Drop a Trigger**

The basic syntax for dropping a trigger is the same as dropping a table or a view:

DROP TRIGGER *TRIGGER_NAME*;

Errors

An error-free design or implementation is one of the ultimate goals in any programming language. You can commit errors by simply not following naming conventions, improperly writing the programming codes (syntax or typo errors like a missing apostrophe or parenthesis) or even when the data entered does not match the data type defined.

To make things easier, SQL has devised a way to return error information so that programmers will be aware of what is going on and be able to undertake the appropriate actions to correct the situation. Some of these error-handling mechanisms are the status parameter SQLSTATE and the WHENEVER clause.

- **SQLSTATE**

　　　　The status parameter or host variable SQLSTATE is an error-handling tool that includes a wide selection of anomalous condition. It is a string that consists of five characters (uppercase letters from A to Z and numerals from 0 to 9), where the first two characters refer to the class code while the next three is the subclass code. The class code identifies the status after an SQL statement has been completed – whether it is successful or not (if not successful, then one of the major types of error conditions are returned). Supplementary information about the execution of the SQL statement is also indicated in the subclass code.

　　　　The SQLSTATE is updated after every operation. If the value is '00000' (five zeroes), it means that the execution was successful and you can proceed to the next operation. If it contains a five-character string other than '00000', then you have to check your programming lines to rectify the error committed. There are numerous ways on how to handle a certain SQL error, depending on the class code and subclass code specified in the SQLSTATE.

- **WHENEVER Clause**

The WHENEVER clause error-handling mechanism focuses on execution exceptions. With this, an error is acknowledged and gives the programmer the option to correct it. This is better than not being able to do something if an error occurs. If you cannot rectify or reverse the error that was committed, then you can just gracefully terminate the application program.

The WHENEVER clause is written before the executable SQL code, specifically in the SQL declaration section. The basic syntax is:

WHENEVER *CONDITION ACTION*;

CONDITION – value can either be SQLERROR (returns TRUE if SQLSTATE class code is other than 00, 01 or 02) or NOT FOUND (returns TRUE if SQLSTATE is 02000)

ACTION – value can either be CONTINUE (execution of the program is continued normally) or GOTO address (execution of a designated program address)

In this chapter, you have learned the primary role of cursors, how triggers work and the importance of handling errors in SQL programming. Learning these advance topics is one step closer in maximizing the potentials of your SQL implementations.

Chapter Twelve: Exercises

Exercise #1

Create an invoice table named **OrderInvoice_TBL** in SQLiteStudio with the following fields:

InvoiceID – primary key, integer data type

CustomerID – integer data type

OrderID – integer data type

TaxAmt – decimal data type with a precision of 9 and a scale of 2

TotalSaleAmt – decimal data type with a precision of 9 and a scale of 2

ShippingFee – decimal data type with a precision of 9 and a scale of 2

Exercise #2

After creating the **OrderInvoice** table, populate the fields using the INSERT statement with the following data values:

Invoice ID	Customer ID	Order ID	Tax Amount	Total Sales	Shipping Fee
2016001	1	1005	$523.80	$198023.05	$1981.78
2016002	3	1006	$302.83	$198302.03	$2005.10
2016003	3	1007	$217.02	$20021.70	$1983.12
2016004	2	1008	$909.00	$200009.09	$19827.22

Exercise #3

Create a view named **OrderLargeSales_VW** from OrderInvoice table where the total sales is greater than $150,000.00 and the tax amount is less than $600. The view will only consist of the following fields: Customer ID, Order ID, Tax Amount and Total Sales.

Exercise #4

Delete the **OrderInvoice_TBL** table and the **OrderInv_VW** view using the DML command DROP.

Exercise Answers

Answers for Exercise #1

1. Launch SQLiteStudio. Click on TOOLS menu and then choose OPEN SQL EDITOR option.

2. Click the QUERY tab at the right and type the following programming lines:

   CREATE TABLE OrderInvoice_TBL (
       InvoiceID   INTEGER PRIMARY KEY,
       CustomerID INTEGER ,
       OrderID   INTEGER,
       TaxAmt   DECIMAL(9, 2),
       TotalSaleAmt DECIMAL(9, 2),
       ShippingFee DECIMAL(9, 2)
   );

3. Click the EXECUTE QUERY button.

Answers for Exercise #2

1. Launch SQLiteStudio. Click on TOOLS menu and then choose OPEN SQL EDITOR option.

2. Click the QUERY tab at the right and type the following programming lines:

   INSERT INTO OrderInvoice_TBL
      VALUES
      (2016001, 1, 1005, 523.80, 198023.05, 1981.78),
      (2016002, 3, 1006, 302.83, 198302.03, 2005.10),
      (2016003, 3, 1007, 217.02, 20021.70, 1983.12),
      (2016004, 2, 1008, 909.00, 200009.09, 19827.22);

3. Click the EXECUTE QUERY button.

Answers for Exercise #3

1. Launch SQLiteStudio. Click on TOOLS menu and then choose OPEN SQL EDITOR option.

2. Click the QUERY tab at the right and type the following programming lines:

   CREATE VIEW OrderInv_VW AS
        SELECT CustomerID, OrderID, TaxAmt, TotalSaleAmt
        FROM OrderInvoice_TBL
        WHERE TotalSaleAmt > 150000 AND TaxAmt < 600;

Answers for Exercise #4

1. Launch SQLiteStudio. Click on TOOLS menu and then choose OPEN SQL EDITOR option.

2. Click the QUERY tab at the right and type the following programming lines to delete the table:

   DROP TABLE OrderInvoice_TBL;

3. Click the EXECUTE QUERY button .

4. To delete the view, type the following programming lines and then click the EXECUTE QUERY button .

   DROP VIEW OrderInv_VW;

Here is a quick recap of what we covered, in case you need a refresher on a certain step:

1. You now have an understanding of the history and uses of the SQL language.
2. You learned how to describe relational databases and database management systems.
3. You learned how to use the different SQL command types and install SQLiteStudio.
4. You learned how to define and use the various data types.
5. You learned how to use the CREATE, ALTER and DROP statements.
6. You learned how to use the INSERT, UPDATE and DELETE statements.
7. You learned how to use the SELECT, WHERE, ORDER BY and GROUP BY statements.
8. You learned how to use the COMMIT, ROLLBACK and SAVEPOINT commands.
9. You also learned how to define, create and drop views.
10. You learned how to assign primary and foreign keys, create indexes and normalize databases.
11. You learned how to use cursors, triggers and errors.

Final Words

I hope that you have truly enjoyed learning the essentials of SQL programming and database management using SQLiteStudio through this eBook. I made sure that you will tremendously benefit from reading this, by meeting your goals in understanding what SQL database is, at an affordable price. I am sure that with the knowledge you have gained through the guidelines of this eBook, you can now plan, design and create your very own databases in SQLiteStudio.

You may also consider learning other programming languages, your knowledge of SQL Programming will give you a tremendous advantage if you wish to learn other languages. You can find other popular programming books by visiting >> http://amzn.to/1Xxmab2

By the way, I would greatly appreciate if you can provide any constructive feedback or reviews that will further improve my skills as a writer. Please feel free to send me an email, especially if you have anything to clarify or ask (even if you just want to drop by and say hello!). My email address is Felix_Alvaro@mail.com.

Before You Go, Here Are Other Books Our Readers Loved!

#1 Best Seller in Mathematical Set Theory

Learn JavaScript Programming Today With This Easy Step-By-Step Guide!

Buy now with 1-Click®

http://amzn.to/1mBhUYM

Best Seller in Popular Counting & Numeration

Learn Python Programming Today With This Easy, Step-By-Step Guide!

Buy now with 1-Click®

http://amzn.to/1WOBiy2

Learn Java Programming Today With This Easy, Step-By-Step Guide!

Buy now with 1-Click®

http://amzn.to/1WTgUw0

Learn AngularJS Web-App Developing Today With This Easy, Step-By-Step Guide

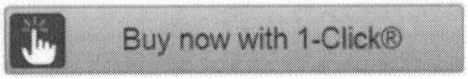

★★★★★

http://amzn.to/1pDq0BZ

Learn R Programming With This Easy, Step-By-Step Guide

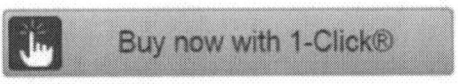

★★★★★

http://amzn.to/24XxoLM

Best Seller in Fiber Optics Engineering

Learn The Linux Operating System and Command Line Today!

Buy now with 1-Click®

http://amzn.to/1QzQPkY

Learn C Programming Today With This Easy, Step-By-Step Guide

Buy now with 1-Click®

http://amzn.to/1Wl6fHu

#1 Best Seller in Functional Analysis

All You Need To Learn To Drive Tons Of Traffic To Your Website Today!

★★★★★

Buy now with 1-Click®

http://amzn.to/21HWFWb

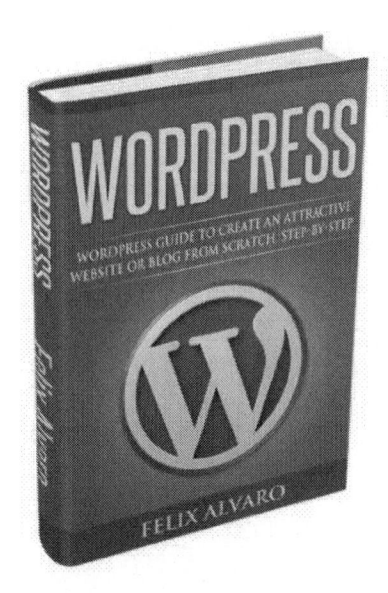

#1 Best Seller in Web Site Design

Easily Create Your Own Eye-Catching, Professional Website or Blog Using WordPress Today!

Buy now with 1-Click®

http://amzn.to/1VHtxZi

Best Seller in Business Insurance

Launch Your Own Profitable eBay Business- Learn Everything You Need to Know to Get Started Today!

Buy now with 1-Click®

http://amzn.to/1R1vnCP

Again, thank you and God bless!

Felix Alvaro

Printed in Poland
by Amazon Fulfillment
Poland Sp. z o.o., Wrocław